KINGDOM WISDOM

The quest for knowledge and wisdom

PHILEMON TSHIKOTA

ISBN: 9781980880165

CONTENTS

Foreword by Dr Sandra Withers
5

Acknowledgements
8

Introduction
9

Chapter 1 - Understanding Wisdom
14

Chapter 2 - Knowing Jesus and His Saving Power
30

Chapter 3 - Sufficiency in Jesus
44

Chapter 4 - The Kingdom of God
59

Chapter 5 - The Holy Spirit
73

Chapter 6 - Passing the Test
88

Chapter 7 - Unfeigned Faith
103

Chapter 8 - Fellowship
133

Chapter 9 - The Call of God
148

Chapter 10 - Attitude
157

Chapter 11 - Dominion
177

Chapter 12 - Ministry
192

Chapter 13 - Prosperity
203

Chapter 14 - Grace and Favour
225

Chapter 15 - Managing People
234

Chapter 16 - The Glory of the City of God
245

Chapter 17 - Building a Good Society with God
249

Chapter 18 - Wisdom Reflections
270

FOREWORD

This book by Philemon Tshikota with the enthralling title, Kingdom Wisdom, is about the acknowledgement and distinction of the wisdom of God, and how indispensable it is to all people. The wisdom of God extends beyond the human mind. Sophia (σοφία, Greek for "wisdom") is a central idea in Hellenistic philosophy and Christian mysticism. The wisdom of God is unsurpassed and infinite, and is vastly superior to human reasoning.

The author elucidates a fresh look at the wisdom of God in a Kingdom setting. The Kingdom of God is the rule of an eternal, sovereign God over the entire universe. Several passages of Scripture show that God is the undeniable Monarch of all creation. "The LORD has established his throne in heaven, and his kingdom rules over all" (Psalm 103:19).

Wisdom is intertwined in knowledge and cannot exist without it. But wisdom is not just knowledge, but "know how." God's wisdom enables people to be insightful. It gives them the "know how" to achieve in life. Wisdom entails the skilfulness to formulate plans and carry them out in the best and most effective way.

There remains much frustration and disappointment in the wisdom of men. New approaches have been sort after but often scrutinized as it pertains to earthly wisdom. In recent times, there has been an overwhelming glut of wisdom-seekers, who still attests to dissatisfaction. The sheer volume of this increasing search for wisdom is staggering. The challenge for most people is the ability to tap into the God-Kind of wisdom which only comes from the person of Jesus Christ.

With this seminal book, Philemon Tshikota is encouraging readers to embrace the essence of God's wisdom, what it is, as well as how to obtain it, walk in it, and align themselves with it. It is God's eternal purpose to reveal wisdom to His people; however, many still lack understanding and revelation. This obvious lack of understanding affects the way people think and act including their attitude, faith and relationship with God.

In this riveting book, the wisdom of the Lord is revealed in each of the eighteen Chapters. It stresses and support readers to commit to wisdom and the weight of God's glory. Apart from the Bible, I cannot think of a better guide to wisdom than the contents of this book. It would allow readers the opportunity to know and experience the wisdom of God that benefits the Kingdom of God on Earth and ultimately in Heaven.

Dr. Sandra Withers
Co-Pastor
Fellowship Community Church
Long Beach, California

ACKNOWLEDGEMENTS

First and foremost, I would like to thank my God for giving me the power to write and put this book together. I could never have done this without Jesus, the author and the finisher of my faith.

To my spiritual father, Pastor Alph Lukau: I can barely explain the tremendous impact his love and wisdom has had in my life. As a father, a leader and a coach, you have helped me through my journey, and groomed me to be a leader. Your passion and determination are inspiring.

To my family: I thank you all so much for your love, support and encouragement. Thank you for believing in me, with such an amazing grit and patience. Love you always and forever.

I would like to thank my friend, Tonny Bio, for helping me publish this book. Thank you so much for your wonderful succour. I sincerely appreciate it.

INTRODUCTION

We are living in a world that is inveigled by a system which is designed to control the thoughts, perceptions, attitudes and behaviours of people. This system is the machinery of the kingdom of this world, which is headed by Satan. The agenda of this system is to sow seeds of destruction in people's lives, in order to ultimately annul the will and the plans of God for them. That is why it is correct to say that there is only two sources of all that we see happening in the lives of people on earth; it is either God or Satan. All the confusions, corruption, hatred, greed, competition, jealousy, envy, and all evil we see are the fruits of the spirit of satan.

To put it more succinctly and plainly I would say any one who is operating through the wisdom of this world is under the influence of the system of Satan. And that is because the wisdom of this world is in enmity with the wisdom of God and it is inspired by Satan himself. The greatest enemies of the system of this world are love and faith, because in the kingdom of God they are of the utmost importance. The greatest factor of maturity in the kingdom is love and the greatest law in the kingdom is the law of faith. That is why satan hates love and faith. So the best thing anyone in the kingdom can do is to pursue love and to fight the good fight of faith.

The chief aim of the world system is to condition the minds and thoughts of people to oppose the wisdom and the will of God. Through the manipulations of Satan, many forsake what is glorious for what is temporal. Look at how he manipulated Eve! Genesis 3:5-6, says, "And the serpent said unto the woman, ye shall not surely die: For God doth know that in the day ye eat thereof, then your eyes shall be opened, and ye shall be as gods, knowing good and evil. And when the woman saw that the tree *was* good for food, and that it *was* pleasant to the eyes, and a tree to be desired to make *one* wise, she took of the fruit thereof, and did eat," The tree looked good for food (the lust of the flesh), and pleasant in her eyes (the lust of the eyes), but that did not change the truth that God said they must not eat it. Satan further manipulated her by telling her that eating the fruit would make one wise, and this has to do with pride of life.

In 1 John 2:16John said, "For all that is in the world, the **lust of the flesh**, and **the lust of the eyes,** and **the pride of life**, is not of the Father, but is of the world." These are three weakness of the human nature that satan used to tempt Eve. These three things are the enemies of faith, love, patience, humility, hope and everything aligned with the Spirit of God.

Satan tried to use the same strategy against Jesus; "And the devil said to Him, 'If you are the Son of God, command this stone to become bread.' But Jesus answered him, saying, "It is written, 'Man shall not live by bread alone, but by every word of God.'" Then the devil, taking Him up on a high mountain, showed Him all the kingdoms of the world in a moment of time. And the devil said to Him, "All this authority I will give you, and their glory; for *this* has been delivered to me, and I give it to whomever I wish. Therefore, if you will worship before me, all will be yours." And Jesus answered and said to him, "Get behind Me, Satan! For it is written, 'You shall worship the Lord your God, and Him only you shall serve.' " Then he brought Him to Jerusalem, set Him on the pinnacle of the temple, and said to Him, "If you are the Son of God, throw yourself down from here. For it is written: 'He shall give His angels charge over you, to keep you,' and, 'in *their* hands they shall bear you up, lest you dash your foot against a stone.'" And Jesus answered and said to him, "It has been said, 'You shall not tempt the Lord your God.'" - Luke 4:3-12.

Jesus demonstrated that we can overcome the schemes of satan against our destinies through the word and the wisdom of God. In order to prevail, win, align with God and fulfil our purposes on earth, we need the wisdom of God. The wisdom of God opens the *door* and paves the *way* for the anointing to flow. Where there is wisdom the favour of God will manifest. That is why the Word says wisdom is the principal thing.-Proverbs 4:7. Wisdom is involved in every area of life; in relationships, in ministry, in finances and in the fulfilment of our purposes.

The level of your success in the fulfilment of your purpose depends on the level of the wisdom of God manifesting in your life. Wisdom is not just about aiming high or being ambitious to get somewhere, but it is about possessing understanding and applying the truth of God in one's life. This begins with the fear of God, which leads us to honour His truth. To know Jesus and to submit to His righteousness is to receive wisdom, and to grow in the knowledge of Him is to grow in wisdom and understanding. But whoever is operating with the wisdom of this world will struggle to see the manifestation of the power and glory of God in his/ her life. Through this book I am sharing God's wisdom on a wide spectrum of subjects that concern our lives daily.

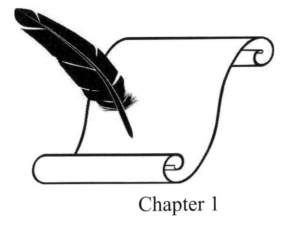

Chapter 1

UNDERSTANDING WISDOM:

Solomon wrote in the book of proverbs;

"To know wisdom and instruction: to receive the words of understanding; To receive instruction of wisdom, justice, and judgement, and equity; To give subtly to the simple, to the young man knowledge and discretion."- (ref: proverbs 1:2-3).

According to the quotation above the Wisdom of God is characterised by justice (fairness/ righteousness in judgement), judgement (God's righteous ruling), equity (fairness), discretion (ability to make prudent decisions with knowledge of truth) and knowledge (information of truth).

Wisdom is God's way and God's way is the right way. Bringing all these together I would say, Wisdom is the use of information of truth to reach a righteous conclusion, with the understanding of God's righteousness, in order to follow the right way. It is aligning with God in judgement, by applying His truth, focusing on His righteousness, in order to execute His justice. It is to have good understanding of justice, judgement, equity, knowledge and discretion. Those who do not fear the Lord do not respect all these. That is why in Proverbs 1:7, Solomon says, "The fear of the Lord is the beginning of knowledge: but fools despise wisdom and instruction." But what is the fear of the Lord? In Proverbs 8:13 he says, "The fear of the Lord is to hate evil: pride, and arrogance, and the evil way, and the forward mouth, do I hate." Someone who is full of pride and arrogance in attitude towards others does not know the fear of the Lord, and therefore lacks wisdom.

God proclaimed Himself before Moses in Exodus, saying, "The Lord, The Lord, merciful and gracious, longsuffering and abundant in goodness and truth, keeping mercy for thousands, forgiving iniquity and transgression and sin........."- Exodus 3:6. From this verse I draw seven pillars of wisdom; Mercy, grace, goodness, compassion, truth, patience and faithfulness. God in His abundant mercy and compassion forgives wrong; by grace He gives what we do not deserve; in His patience He bears with man's imperfections; in His truth and goodness He seeks the best even for those who are regarded as nothing by man.

Because He is so merciful He is perfectly fair and just, and He seeks justice and fairness for every man in spite of their position and title in society or anything on the outside.

Solomon wrote and said, "To do justice and judgement is more acceptable to Him than sacrifice."- Proverbs 21:3. When we are merciful we are able to seek justice for everyone, as God does. And a man of wisdom does not tolerate injustice and oppression of others. In proverbs 20:28 he says, "Mercy and truth preserve the king: and his throne is upheld by mercy." That means the governance of one who rules over people is strengthened and prospered by his merciful heart towards the people.

Jesus in Matthew 9:13 said, "Go and learn what this means, I desire mercy, not sacrifice."-. Matthew 12:19 says, "He shall not strive, nor cry; neither shall any man hear his voice in the streets. A bruised reed shall he not break, and smoking flax shall he not quench, till he send forth judgement unto victory." This shows us that Jesus does not seek justice for someone because the person seems honourable; but He seeks justice equally, even for the weak, the broken, and the forsaken.

Where there is God's judgement there is justice and He will cause justice to win.

All of us want to resist injustice against our own selves and we condemn it if it is practised against us or if we are affected by it. But often when a man is set over others, before you know it you begin to see injustice manifesting through him, against others. God has never had any man's hand upon Him or someone ruling over Him to correct Him; yet He has never been unjust or unfair towards any man who is high or is low. His justice is not like man's justice. His justice is characterised by mercy and compassion for all men. It culminates through the gift of righteousness that he has given through the death of Jesus His Son.

Solomon in proverbs 3:3 says, "Let not mercy and truth forsake thee: bind them about thy neck; write them upon the table of thine heart." He speaks of mercy and truth. Mercy is the greatest characteristic of God's love. The truth is the absolute and perfect will of God, His thoughts, and all He says concerning the past, present and future. Solomon is encouraging us to seek mercy and truth. Proverbs 21:21 says, "He that followeth after righteousness and mercy findeth life, righteousness and honour."

The Truth is God's Wisdom, and when you have the knowledge of it you speak boldly and without wavering or fearing anything, because it liberates you. Proverbs 22:20 says, "Have not I written to you the excellent things in counsels and knowledge. That I might make thee know the certainty of the words of truth; that thou mightiest answer the words of truth to them that send unto thee." With knowledge of truth Elihu boldly opened his mouth and said, "My words shall be of the uprightness of my heart: and my lips shall utter knowledge clearly. If thou can answer me, set thy words in order before me, stand up" In Job 33:3-5. What really moves me is that this man spoke with such confidence when the situation at hand was way above human understanding and they didn't know what to make of it.

Elihu revealing the righteousness of God to Job closes by saying, "Touching the Almighty, we can not find Him out: He is excellent in power and in judgement and in plenty of justice: He will not afflict. Men therefore fear Him: He respecteth not any that are wise of heart.- Job 37:23. In Job 34:19, Elihu shows us that God does not accept the person of princes, nor does He regard the rich more that the poor? For they are all the works of His hands."

The problem with Job was that during his trials he focused on his own integrity rather than the righteousness of God. His friends also condemned him because they focused on his righteousness rather than the righteousness of God. When you focus on God's righteousness you can not judge or condemn anyone. There will be no reason for judgement, condemnation, competition, strife, wrath, envy, jealousy and fighting.

We are not looking for people who will say, "Do you know me? Have you seen me?" We need people who will say, "Have you seen the righteousness of God?" We are saved to lift up the righteousness of God, who is merciful, fair and just. This is what Elihu did. He said, "I will fetch my knowledge from afar, and will ascribe righteousness to my Maker."-Job 36:3; (psalm 71:15, 16, 19, 24). Psalm 40:10 says, "I have not hid thy righteousness within my heart; I have declared thy faithfulness and thy salvation: I have not concealed thy loving kindness and thy truth from the great congregation." When God started addressing Job He took him to the beginning. He says, "Where were you when I laid the foundation of the earth? "-Job 38:4. This brings into our minds the knowledge that God purposed everything in the beginning, in His perfect righteousness, according to His perfect will, without anyone to instruct Him. He can not be unfair to anyone because He started everything before any of us was there.

All these reveal to us the nature of God who breathes justice and righteousness. And Paul in 1 Corinthians 12:31, says, "Yet I show you a more excellent way." This way that Paul is talking about is love. Love is not what God does, it is who He is.

Seeking Wisdom:

- **Allow God to teach you**: Proverbs 1:23- "Turn you at my reproof; behold, I will pour out my spirit unto you, I will make known my words unto you."

- **Submit to God and Honour Him**: Proverbs 1:7-"The fear of the Lord is the beginning of knowledge; but fools despise wisdom and instruction."

- **Desire wisdom and make time to seek it**: Proverbs 18:1-"Through desire a man, having separated himself, seeketh and intermeddleth with all wisdom."

- **Be thirsty for wisdom**: Proverbs 2:3-4-"Yea, if thou, criest after knowledge, and liftest up thy voice for understanding; If thou seekest her as silver, and searchest for her as for hid treasures;" Psalm 84-"My soul longeth, yea, even fainteth for the courts of the Lord: my heart and my flesh crieth out for the living God

- **Pursue mercy and truth**: Proverbs 3:3-"Let not mercy and truth forsake thee: bind them about thy neck: write them upon the table of thine heart."

Why we need Wisdom (Reasons for seeking Wisdom):

Proverbs 3:1-2
"My son, forget not my law; but let thine heart keep my commandments: For length of days, and long life, and peace shall they add to thee."

Proverbs 3:13-20
"Happy is the man that findeth wisdom and the man that getteth understanding. For the merchandise of it is better than the merchandise of silver and the gain thereof than fine gold. She is more precious than rubies: and all the things thou canst desire are not to be compared unto her. Length of days is in her right hand and in her left hand riches and honour. Her ways are ways of pleasantness, and all her path are peace. She is a tree of life to them that lay hold upon her: and happy is everyone that retaineth her. The Lord by wisdom hath founded the earth: by understanding hath he established the heavens."

Proverbs 24:3
"Through wisdom is an house builded; and by understanding it is established. And by knowledge

shall the chamber be filled with all precious and pleasant riches."

Proverbs 4:7-9
"Wisdom is the principal thing; therefore get wisdom: and with all thy getting get understanding. Exalt her and she shall promote thee: and she shall bring thee to honour, when thou dost embrace her. She shall give to thine head an ornament of grace; a crown of glory shall she deliver to thee."

What happens when you find Wisdom?

Proverbs 2:5
"Then shalt thou understand the fear of the Lord, and find the knowledge of God."

Proverbs 2:9
"Then shalt thou understand righteousness, and judgement, and equity: yea, every good path. When wisdom entereth into thine heart and knowledge is pleasant unto thy soul: Discretion shall preserve thee, understanding shall keep thee. To deliver thee from the way of the evil man, from the man that speakest forward things;"

Proverbs 3:4
"*And* so find favor and high esteem in the sight of God and man.."

God Reigns with Justice and Righteousness:

The psalmist says, "justice and judgement are the habitation of thy throne: Mercy and truth shall go before thy face."-Psalm 89:14. God honours those that love justice, but He deeply dislikes oppression. Elihu in Job 34:26, says, "He striketh them as wicked men in the open sight of others; Because they turned their back from Him and would not consider any of His ways (His motives, thoughts, desires, will): So that they cause the cry of the poor to come unto Him and He heareth the cry of the afflicted." The psalmist in Psalm 82:3 says, "Defend the poor and fatherless: do justice to the afflicted and needy. Deliver the poor and needy: rid them out of the hand of the hand of the wicked. They know not, neither do they understand: they walk on in the darkness: all the foundations of the earth are out of course. I have said ye are gods: and all of you are the children of the Most High. But ye shall die like men and fall like one of the princes."

Proverbs 21:12 says, "The righteous man wisely considereth the house of the wicked: but God overthroweth the house of the wicked for his wickedness." Perhaps one of the good questions one can ask here is, who is Solomon referring to when he says the wicked? Proverbs 21:10 says, "The soul of the wicked desireth evil: his neighbour findeth no favour in his eyes." Proverbs 21:7 says, "The robbery of the wicked shall destroy them;

because they refuse to do judgement." That means the nature of the wicked is manifested by his attitude towards others. He hates justice and he is never gracious.

Jesus in Matthew 6:33, says, "But seek ye first the kingdom of God, and His righteousness; and all these things shall be added unto you." His righteousness is manifested and proven in us when He justifies us through faith apart from our works, by grace, according to His will. But His righteousness is manifested through us towards others when we pursue mercy, love, compassion and grace towards them. To seek His righteousness is to seek His mercy, love, compassion and grace towards all of us. We become effectively profitable to God when we pursue His mercy and compassion towards others and when we desire to see His will done in their life. And above all, the most important thing you can do is to love God with all your heart- that is where it all begins. That is why our assignments in life are birthed from love. By Him we are empowered to love and love conquers all things. The kingdom of God speaks of His will, and His righteousness speaks of His fairness and justice.

Before Jesus started His ministry He went to the Jordan River to be baptised by John. John forbade him saying, I have need to be baptised of you. But Jesus said to him, "Suffer it to be so now: for thus it becometh us to fulfil all righteousness." John the Baptist felt that he was neither worthy nor qualified to baptise Jesus. As a matter of fact, you could bring Moses, Samuel, Elisha, Job, Abraham or Isaiah. None of them would qualify by works to baptise Jesus. It was not a matter of qualifying because if any one would try to qualify he would do so through human effort. When John baptised Jesus it was not man and God seeking to fulfil the righteousness of man. It was man and God working together to manifest/ demonstrate the righteousness of God. The baptism of John was a baptism unto repentance and it was signifying the turning of the hearts of men to God. Jesus had no need for repentance; no need for baptism of repentance. He was tempted at all points, yet without sin. He couldn't carry the sins of the world if He Himself had any sin. God took the sins of the world and put them on the lamb that was pure.

The righteousness of God manifested was this that God in His greatness humbled Himself to come as a man, to serve man, living among man and chose to submit Himself to the authority given to a man (John) to baptise people. He was 100 percent God but lived in a body that was 100 percent the body of man. He didn't eat food brought by angels, He used boats of man, lived in a house as man and put on clothe made of hands of man. Man was supposed to pay the price for his own sin and the price was eternal death. So God came as a man in order to take the sin of man and paid the price for the sins of man in the flesh. Jesus was not going to carry the sins of man as God but as a man. So Jesus contained Himself in humility and allowed John to baptise Him as he was baptising every man. Romans 3:26, says, "To declare, I say, at this time His righteousness: that He might be just and the justifier of him that believe in Jesus." Not that He is trying to be just but that His justice may be manifested. That means John was justified and qualified by God, through faith, to baptise Jesus. And therein is the righteousness and goodness of God manifested.

Look at the faithfulness and righteousness of God. He promised Abraham that He would make him a father of many nations. Because of that, Abraham obeyed God by faith. Later God asked him to sacrifice his own son, without giving him any reason why. Abraham in obedience purposed to do as God said, believing that God was able to raise up his son from the dead. So by faith he was willing to give up his own son to God and believed that God has power to resurrect him. This is finally what God did for us. He gave up His own son and resurrected Him on the third day. And because Abraham was willing and ready to do what God did, today God and Abraham are reaping the same reward.

Whoever receives Jesus in his life is called both a child of God and a child of Abraham.

Let us look at what the Word says is not Wisdom from God:

James 3:14-16 says, "But if ye have bitter envying and strife in your hearts, glory not, and lie not against the truth. This wisdom descendeth not from above, but is earthly, sensual, devilish. For where envying and strife is, there is confusion and every evil work." According to the truth of God envy and strife are associated with pride and are not aligned with the wisdom of God. They are not the fruits of God's spirit.

James further explains the character of a wise person. In James 3:13 he says, "Who is a wise man and endued with knowledge among you? let him shew out of a good conversation his works with meekness of wisdom." He uses the word meekness which is associated with patience, humility, gentleness and being submissive. In James 3:17-18, he says, " But the wisdom that is from above is first pure then peaceable, gentle, willing to yield, full of mercy and good fruits, without partiality and without hypocrisy. Now the fruit of righteousness is sown in peace by those who make peace." That means if it is wisdom from God it will align with purity (From inside out), peace, gentleness, mercy,

agreeableness, justice/fairness, sincerity and whatever is the fruit of the Spirit of God.

Prudence (Practical Wisdom)

Proverbs 4:25

**"Let thine eyes look right on, and let thine eyelids
look straight before thee. Ponder the path of thy
feet, and let thine ways be established. Turn not to
the right hand nor to the left: remove thy foot
from evil."** To achieve this, we must focus on the
word of God and avoid distractions. Live every day
with a mission. Add to your good/ godly intentions
wise choices and decisions. Do not give your
attention to just anyone or anything. Do not be lead
astray. You have a purpose to fulfil in your life.
Maintain your focus. It is better to be hated by
people than to be distracted. Let your interactions
be aligned with your mission and vision. Don't
invite distractions and don't answer to distractions.
"Focus and be diligent". Be diligent with the details.
Maximise your time and potential. Take your
motives, intentions, mission and vision seriously

Proverbs 16:3

**"Commit thy works unto the Lord, and thy
thoughts shall be established."**
We must commit what we do (our actions), our
choices and decisions to the Lord. Many of us want
to commit to God what we want to achieve, by
telling Him or asking Him to bring it to pass, but we

do not want to commit to the Lord the steps of getting there. God wants us to see the picture in our heart and then commit our steps of getting there, to Him, so that He can direct us. We must acknowledge Him to lead us. Proverbs 16:9 says, "A man's heart deviseth His way: but the Lord directeth His steps." It is for a man to see in his heart the picture of what he wants, but God guides him every step of the way, showing him the right choices to make. We are not suppose to tell Him what we want and then direct our own way. That is why Psalm 37:23 says, "The steps of a good man are ordered by the Lord: and he delighteth in his way." This is one of the things that happen when God rebukes the devourer. He directs us away from choices that will cause us to lose our resources into the hand of the devourer.

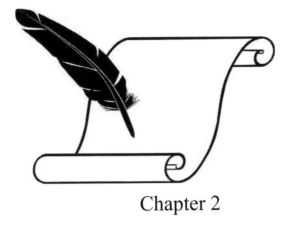

Chapter 2

KNOWING JESUS CHRIST AND HIS SAVING POWER:

The most important question any one can ever ask in life is, "who is Jesus"? To know Jesus is to have wisdom and to have understanding. To grow in the knowledge of Him is to grow in wisdom and understanding. Elihu said, "Great men are not always wise; neither do the aged understand judgement."-Job 32:9. The proof of this is Pharaoh who was regarded one of the most powerful kings of his time. In Exodus 5:2 Pharaoh said, "Who is the

Lord, that I should obey His voice to let Israel go? I know not the Lord, neither will I let Israel go." Nebuchadnezzar also was full of pride, and God drove him from men and caused him to eat grass as oxen. Afterwards God restored him, his glory and his honour. And in Daniel 4:37, Nebuchadnezzar says, "Now I Nebuchadnezzar praise and extol and honour the king of heaven, all whose works are truth, and his ways judgement: and those that walk in pride he is able to abase."

Jesus said to His disciples, "He that has seen me has seen the Father."- John 13:9. Here Jesus was not referring to them seeing His physical body, but His ways. By His ways I mean His attitude, the thoughts of His heart, His motives, His goodness, His love, His holiness and His nature in totality. Hebrews 1:3 shows us that Jesus is the brightness of the glory of the Father and the express image of His person. So to know Jesus is to know His heart and to know His heart is to know the heart of the Father. To know His ways is to know the ways of the Father. And to have understanding in life is to know Jesus and to walk in the fear/ honour of Him. The scripture also teaches us that, He was in the bosom of the Father.- John 1:18. Meaning, no one knows the Father like Him. In fact Jesus said, "Neither knoweth any man the Father, save the Son, and he to whomsoever the Son will reveal Him."-Matthew 11:27. No one knows the Heart of the Father but the Son and whomsoever the Son will reveal His Heart to.

One famous definition of who Jesus is, by Jesus Himself, is, "I am the way, the life and the truth."- John 14:6. He is the way and the only way to the Father. Acts 4:12 says, "Salvation is found in no one else, for there is no other name under heaven given to mankind by which we must be saved." That says it all. Without salvation no one can come to the Father. And salvation is only possible through Jesus, who has paid the full price for our sins on the cross. Apart from Him there is no hope for salvation. The best any one can do on earth is not close to being enough to give him salvation.

Jesus is like a rich man who walks into a court room to take the place of someone who is judged and sentenced for life in prison, and gives the man an inheritance in His wealth. He is not there to discuss the crime the man committed but to take away the death sentence from him and to give him an inheritance from his wealth. Whether it is hard to believe or not that is our reality. All this is because of His love, mercy and grace, which is unsearchable to human mind. His justice is manifested when He justifies and blesses those who believe in Jesus, apart from their own works.

The second thing He said is, "the life." Colossians 1:19 says, "For it pleased the Father that in him should all fullness dwell." All the life that is in the Father is in Jesus. When Jesus came He came with the best of God's treasures in Him. Through Him God gave us His best gift in abundance. That is the gift of life. Jesus is the gift of life. The life that flows from Jesus is in abundance. He says, "I am come that they might have life and that they might have it more abundantly."-John 10:10. In the scripture at the top of this paragraph He says, "I am the life." That means if you touch Him you have touched life. If He breathes into you, life has breathed into you. If you have Him you have life in abundance. When God gave us Jesus He gave us life in abundance. Life is everything that is found in God. When all that is in God is taken away from a man he dies spiritually, though His body be alive. To receive life in abundance means that all that is in God has come into us. He did not just give us a bit of Himself, but He came into us. He says we and Him are one. That means we are also able to breathe life where there is death. We have power to speak life because we have life in abundance. We must be conscious of that. God Himself has made a dwelling in us as a man dwells in a house. He takes care of His house better than a man would take care of his house.

The third thing He is, by His own testimony, is "the truth". The truth is the absolute and perfect will of God and all He says concerning the past present and future. Jesus is the Word of God and He is the truth. He teaches us the perfect will of the Father. In John 8:32 He says, "Then you shall know the truth and the truth shall make you free." That means Jesus is the truth that makes us free. He gives us knowledge that makes us free. This freedom is not for our spirits. When we received Jesus God gives birth to us in the Spirit. We are freed from the power of darkness and taken away from the kingdom of satan. In the spirit we are seated in the heavenly places with Jesus from the time we are born again. We have power and authority. We are kings and priests. The freedom we need is for our minds and our souls. That means though in the spirit we have abundant life we may not fully manifest that life in the physical realm if our minds and souls are not converted or freed. James 1:21, shows that the Word is able to save our souls. Psalm 19:7, says, "The law of the Lord is perfect, converting the soul: the testimony of the Lord is sure, making wise the simple." The Word brings transformation in our souls, so that we may not walk conforming to this world. Simply put, freedom manifests when our souls and minds are free. That is why it is hard trying to oppress someone who is free in the mind.

Psalm 119:45, says, "I will walk at liberty: for I seek thy precepts." This scripture shows us that when we seek and find the truth, which is in the Word, which is Jesus, we are able to walk at liberty. When He says you shall know the truth and the truth will make you free, it is not just a slogan to make you feel good. The word helps us to walk at liberty, with no hindrance; nothing pulling us back. When the truth starts to shine in your mind and soul, there are certain prayers you used to pray for long, that you will stop praying, because of the revelation of the truth. You will begin to change your attitude to conform to that of Jesus. When we received Jesus we received everything pertaining to life and godliness, but without understanding we can walk as if we have nothing. The scripture says, "Whatsoever thing is born of God overcomes the world."- 1 John 5:4. That means, whatever is born of God has everything in itself to overcome the world. If our minds can not through knowledge align with that, we can walk thinking the enemy has the upper hand; as though we do not have what it takes to overcome. In Christ is all the knowledge we need to be everything we were born to be.

Because Jesus is the Truth, the Word and the Wisdom of God, He is able to give us wisdom and set us high through wisdom. In psalm 119:98, the psalmist says, "Thou through thy commandments hast made me wiser than mine enemies: for they are ever with me. I have more understanding than all my teachers: for thy testimonies are my meditation. I understand more than the ancients, because I keep thy precepts." What this man is saying is that he has knowledge and understanding that is above what experience can give. This is wisdom that a man can not be taught. It is only given by Jesus Himself. Elihu is Job 32:9 said, "Great men are not always wise: neither do the aged understand judgement." This means that wisdom is not found in a man just because he is called a great man or has many years of experience. Many people when they mentor you and guide you will use knowledge they obtained through their experience. But there is knowledge that Jesus gives that is above what experience can teach a man.

Jesus gives us wisdom that the world is not able to resist. In Luke 21:15, says, "For I will give you a mouth and wisdom, which all your adversaries shall not be able to gainsay or resist." Acts 6:9, says, "There arose certain of the synagogue, which is called the synagogue of the Libertines, and

Cyrenians, and Alexandrians, and of them of Cilicia and of Asia, disputing with Stephen. And they were not able to resist the wisdom and spirit by which he spake." This Stephen was not even part of the twelve apostles who were solely devoted to the ministry of the word. He was one of those who were assigned to serve the tables; he was in the ministry of serving the widows, because they were trying to make sure that the widows were not neglected. So the twelve apostles had asked that seven men be chosen to assist with that and Stephen was one of them. But Stephen was full of faith and the Holy Ghost.

The Blood of Jesus:

On the cross of calvary, as Jesus hang between heaven and earth, the price was fully paid for our sins. When He died on the cross the veil that had closed the holy of holies was torn from top to bottom. In heaven Jesus entered into the holy of holies with His blood for our atonement. The blood of Jesus allows us access to the holy of holies, to come boldly before the throne of grace. Hebrews 9:7, says, "But into the second (tabernacle) went the high priest alone once a year, not without blood, which he offered for himself, and for the errors of people: The Holy Ghost signifying, that the way into the holiest of all was not yet made manifest, while the first tabernacle was still standing:"

Hebrews 9:13, says, "If the blood of bulls and of goats, and the ashes of an heifer sprinkling the unclean sanctifieth to the purifying of the flesh: How much more shall the blood of Chrsit, who through the eternal Spirit offered Himself without spot to God, purge your conscience from dead works to serve the living God." That means the blood of Jesus perfectly frees our conscience from the guilt of trespasses. We honour the power of the blood more than the negative impact of any sin.

Hebrews 10:16, says, "This is the covenant that I will make with them after those days, saith the Lord, I will put my laws into their hearts, and in their minds will I write them: And their sins and iniquities will I remember no more. Now where there is remission of these there is no more offering for sin." In summary what these verses are saying is, the problem of sin has been dealt with. Because sin has been dealt with by the blood of Jesus there is no need to offer sacrifices for sins. We must also not invent other ways to pay the price for our sins because the price has been paid. That is the truth that God wants us to embrace and honour. The blood of Jesus through faith in Jesus renders sin and death powerless to those who believe. Hebrews 12:24 shows us that the blood of Jesus speaks better things than the blood of Abel. Those who believe in Jesus, His blood speaks for them against all the accusations and verdict of satan. Revelations 12:10, says, "They overcame him (satan) by the blood of the lamb and by the word of their testimony."

Redemption:

Redemption is when something or someone that is bound, held captive or under the oppressive rule of someone, is freed and saved from that bondage.

Those of us who are in Christ have hope, because we have already been redeemed from the dominon of sin and death. If sin and death do not reign over then we are free to reign in life, not because we are perfect in works, but because of the power of the redemption of the blood of Jesus. We have been redeemed from the curse of the law. The scripture says, "By the works of the law shall no flesh be justified." That means under the law there is no hope. Psalm 130:8, says, "He shall redeem Israel from all his iniquities." This means that God had a plan to redeem man from the bondage of the inherent nature of sin. The law did not redeem man from sin but made sin more sinful. But through the redemption of Christ we are no longer under the law but under grace. We are not justified by the deeds of the law but by faith, in Christ our redeemer.

Colossians 1:3, says "Who hath delivered us from the power of darkness, and hath translated us into the kingdom of His dear Son: In whom we have redemption through His blood, even the forgiveness of sins:" Our redemption came when we were forgiven our sins and were delivered from the power of darkness. Sin has no power over us and darkness has no power over us. We rejoice knowing that Jesus has overcome for our redemption, justification and salvation and has freely given us power over all the power of the enemy and nothing shall by any means hurt us.

Jesus has redeemed us from death, from sin and has redeemed everything concerning us. Isaiah 53:5 says, "but He was wounded for our transgressions,

He was bruised for our iniquities: the chastisement of our peace was upon Him; and with His stripes we are healed." That means he paid the price through His body for our transgressions and iniquities to be forgiven. He has redeemed our peace and our health. Our peace in every area of our lives has been redeemed. The health of our bodies, souls, families and nations has been redeemed. What we need is to manifest the fruit of the redemption Jesus has done for us.

Sanctification:

The word sanctify in Greek is Hagiazo. It means to separate. It is the sovereign act of God, whereby He sets apart a person, a place or a thing in order to use it for His purpose. Genesis 2:3 says, "And God blessed the seventh day, and sanctified it: because that in it He had rested from all His work which God created and made." God separated and set the seventh day apart because it is the day in which He rested from His work. Until today every where in the world Sunday is day is known as a resting day.

There are three levels of sanctification that we need. The first and most important sanctification is in the spirit. This is the sanctification we receive by grace instantly when we receive Jesus. We are sanctified once for ever in the spirit. The Apostle Peter wrote in 1 Peter 1:2, "Elect according to the foreknowledge of God the Father, through sanctification of the Spirit, unto obedience and sprinkling of the blood of Jesus Christ:" Hebrews 10:14 says, "For by one offering He hath perfected for ever them that are sanctified." Hebrews 10:10

says, "By the which will we are sanctified through the offering of the body of Jesus Christ once for all."

The second sanctification is that of the soul. This one happens through the renewal of our minds by the word of God. John 17:19 says, "And for their sakes I sanctify myself, that they also might be sanctified through the truth." The word of God is for our souls and it sanctifies our souls. To His disciples Jesus said, "Ye are already clean because of the word I have spoken to you." Paul said, "Be transformed by the renewing of your mind."

The last sanctification is of the flesh. 1 Thessalonians 4:3 says, "For this is the will of God, even your sanctification, that ye should abstain from fornication: That every one of you should know how to possess his vessel in sanctification and honour; Not in the lust of concupiscene, even as the Gentiles which know not God:" Our purity in the flesh helps us to stay strong in faith. Sin is one of the enemies of faith and as a result, of the flow also of the anointing.

The Mercies of God:

Isaiah 53:5 says, "But He was wounded for our transgressions, He was bruised for our iniquities: the chastisement of our peace was upon Him; by His stripes we are healed. All we like sheep have gone astray; we have turned every one to his own way; and the Lord hath laid on Him the iniquity of us all." What we see clearly in this scripture is that somebody suffered in the flesh in order for our wrongs to be forgiven. He was wounded, bruised, chastised, and endure stripes as a punishment for our wrongs. We are told that we were all heading to the wrong direction until the Lord redeemed us. We were all heading to hell with the burdens of our sins upon us but the Lord decided in His mercy to take our sins and put them upon Jesus who was perfect enough to be the sacrifice for our trespasses. Jesus has paid the price for our sins, we do not need to pay the price for our sins.

God had compassion and mercy on us. His mercy is far deeper than the human mind can understand. There was nothing that a man could give to be redeemed from sin and death and from the curse of the law. The sacrifice of animals could not redeem us because they did not take away sin nor its remembrance. There was no way for any one to pay the price, even by his own life; it would still be meaningless. But God in His love for us was willing not only to forgive man for his iniquity but also to pay the price Himself for the redemption of our lives. And He sent Jesus to be the life, the way and the truth to us.

God's forgiveness is different from man's forgiveness. In Hebrews 8:12 the Lord says, "For I will forgive their wickedness and will remember their sins no more." The power of His forgiveness has taken away the remembrance of sin. To His disciples Jesus said, "This is what is written: The Christ will suffer and rise from the dead on the third day, and in His name repentance and forgiveness of sins will be proclaimed to all nations, beginning in Jerusalem."-Luke 24:47. Repentance and forgiveness is only preached to all nations because Jesus died and paid the price for our sins.

41

Before He paid the price for sin, there was no place for repentance and no message of forgiveness of sins to proclaim. Concerning Esau Hebrews 12:17 says, "he was rejected: for he found no place of repentance though he sought it carefully with tears." Repentance means turning to submit yourself completely to the righteousness of Jesus, not your own. God's forgiveness towards us means separating us from sin and taking away the remembrance of sin.

God in His love, was compelled by His compassion and mercy to redeem us from our eternal hopelessness, bondage and death. Isaiah 54:6 says, "For the Lord hath called thee as a woman forsaken and grieved in spirit, and a wife of youth, when thou wast refused, saith thy God. For a small moment have I forsaken thee; but with great mercies will I gather thee." In verses 10 and 11, He says, "For the mountains shall depart, and the hills be removed; but my kindness shall not depart from thee, neither shall the covenant of my peace be removed, saith the Lord that hath mercy on thee. O thou afflicted, tossed with tempest, and not comforted, behold, I will lay thy stones with fair colours, and lay thy foundations with sapphires." We see in these verses the expression of God's great compassion and mercy for Israel and His zeal to save them. Thou they had sinned He was zealous to spare them from their suffering and pain.

Through Jesus God has demonstrated His unsearchable mercies towards man kind. In great love He gave Jesus as a sacrifice for our sins and gave us the choice to receive Him in our lives as our

Lord and saviour. All this is because in His mercy He desired to redeem us from eternal death.

God is eternally full of compassion, mercy, grace and goodness. On Mount Sinai God passed by proclaiming before Moses, saying, "The Lord, The Lord, merciful and gracious, longsuffering and abundant in goodness and truth, keeping mercy for thousands, forgiving iniquity and transgression and sin…." This was to give Moses the revelation of the heart and the nature of God.

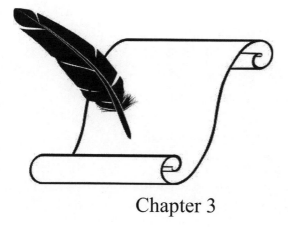

Chapter 3

SUFFICIENCY IN JESUS:

God knows everything and everything that exists came from Him. He knows even our thoughts and everything concerning our future. He is the master planner of our lives from beginning to end, because we came from Him. The help we need in order to fulfil our assignments on earth He knows how to give it to us. There is no one we need more than we need Him. In fact all those whose help will be profitable to Him in your lives are those He equips and sends to us. Even those that He sends to help you, you do not need them like you need Him. There is no one in your life who is a full stop as long as you are aligned with God. That means even if anyone chooses to walk away from me I will still be able to excel without them. The walking away of any one does not bring my life or my assignment and destiny to an end. The more the wrong people walk away the stronger I become.

There are two men in the bible who were rejected by those who could have helped them to fulfil their destinies. But still they fulfilled their destinies without them.

 The first man I want to talk about is David. Saul, the first king of Israel could have been the one to mentor David and to prepare him to be king after him as David had already been anointed. In stead of mentoring and helping David, he hated and persecuted him with envy and jealousy. David had to spend days in the wilderness and in caves and among strangers, away from home because the king wanted him dead. David received no mentorship, no training, and no guidance from Saul, but God Himself trained and prepared him to be king in Israel. David was not a king like Saul because God prepared him to be a different kind of king. In fact concerning David, God said his throne will be forever. In 2 Samuel 23:3, David said, "The God of Israel said, the Rock of Israel spake to me, he that ruleth over men must be just, ruling in the fear of God." Wow! so God was not looking for someone from a perfect family, but someone that was just and would rule in the fear of God.

In 2 Samuel 23:5, David says, "Although my house be not so with God; yet He made with me an everlasting covenant, ordered all things, and sure: for this is all my salvation, and all my desire, although He make it not to grow." Meaning even though the house of David's father had no specific exclusive covenant with God, yet God made a covenant with him. Not just a covenant but an everlasting covenant. Without the help of Saul, God made David the best king, became a reference from generation to generation. God taught David how to rule as a king. King Saul took away David's wife who was his daughter given to David by himself, and he gave her to another man. It was good for David to carry on pursuing God; sometimes people will give you something in order to take away everything from you.

The second man I want to talk about is Joseph. Joseph was envied, hated and sold to be a slave by his own brothers who could have helped and supported him to become who he was born to be. In stead they conspired against him and sold him to be a slave in a foreign country; where he was he could neither get nor claim support of his family. There was no one to stand with him when he was unfairly accused of a crime he did not commit. There was no one to come and visit him when he was in prison. He survived among strangers. There was no one to hold his hand, but God was there with him. God was with him and he exalted him among strangers even when he was in prison. And in the end God promoted him. I believe when he was there as a slave God taught him things he couldn't have leant from his family. So without the help of his family, God trained and helped Joseph prepare for what he had prepared for him.

There is no one on earth that can stop your destiny if you in Christ. Not even those who withhold their help and support from us, no matter how important it is, or any one who stands against us as an enemy. That means with God you are unstoppable. You don't need in life anyone whose heart is not with you. God will send in your life people whose hearts are with Him and will be with you. People can take away everything from you but they can not take away the faithfulness of God from you. He is a covenant keeping God and He honours your faith.

There may be some people you have known who you believed in so much but they didn't believe in you as much. There may be people who no matter how much good you did for them they rewarded you evil for good. Some may have made you feel like you are worth nothing. They may have destroyed your self esteem. Some may have taken advantage of you and some may have rejected you. You probably couldn't see yourself winning without them; or without their help, support and love. You tried, you wished, you hoped and you prayed that things had turned out different. It is important for you to know that there is nothing people can do to stop you, and nothing they did or didn't do, can stop you. There is nothing they owe you that you can not shine without. Whatever bad thought they made you to have of yourself is a lie of the devil. Come back to course because the devil is a liar. Focus on the vision the Lord has given you and who you truly are in Him.

What they did to you back then is not worth carrying into your future. After these trials God will give you a testimony. Let all that bad past be buried behind you. Refuse to let it come back in your life as the walking dead; send it back to the grave. As you believe in yourself and focus on the future, any good thing in you that was buried because of bad past experiences will resurrect.

Let go of every pain and forgive everyone who did you wrong. Expect to see manifestations of the best in your life. Satan loves to use his schemes to entice people into his traps and into trouble. If satan has used people in the past to try and destroy your destiny, it is a shame on him because God has preserved you, strengthened and made you wiser. Forgive and let the past go. Make a decision never to give satan room. Let no one again take you off the path. Let not again satan use anyone to entice you, and drag you into the pit. Let no one again take advantage of you. Don't let satan come and mess up with your destiny.

Ask God for wisdom. Put God's love first in all you do and let Him lead you. If what you experience does not reflect God's love and His will, then it is not good for you. What is of God will give you peace of mind. It will strengthen you even in the lowest of your time. It will happen through God's power and favour; not through natural efforts. You will have no ungodly pressure to perform or to force anything to happen.

Ask God to remove the impact of the memory of any bad experience you had. Allow God to do something new in your life. Let no memory, thought or dream take you back. Don't follow your emotions; follow God's wisdom and love. God will connect you with people whose hearts are sincerely after Him. Those will be the best people in your life; your destiny friends. So don't let the past hold you back.

In Christ we have the gift of abundant life. In Psalm 78:20, he says, "Behold, he smote the rock, that the waters gushed out, and the streams overflowed; can he give bread also? Can he provide flesh for his people?" (Bread/ flesh: the word to build us up. Fellowship: God speaks to build us up). As Moses smote the rock for water to come out, so did it please the Lord to bruise Jesus, in order for us to receive life in abundance. As God smote the rock, which is Jesus, the river of life gushed out and the stream of it overflowed. He did not spare.

In psalm 46 the psalmist says, "God is our refuge and strength, a very present help in trouble. Therefore, will not we fear, though the earth be removed, and though the mountains be carried into the midst of the sea; Though the waters thereof roar and be troubled, though the mountains shake with the swelling thereof. There is a river, the streams whereof shall make glad the city of God, the holy place of the tabernacles of the most High." We are not afraid because the river of life that flows from Jesus is what we live by. This river gives abundance of water and its streams overflow. That means the anointing given to us is meant to overflow. In Revelations 22:17, it says, "The Spirit and the bride say, Come. And let him that is athirst come. And whosoever will, let him take the water of life freely."

Therefore, let no one oppress you or take advantage of you. No one has the power and the right to do so except what you give them. Remember you need nobody in life like you need the Lord Himself. That is why you should fear not the hatred of man. Any one who has something that you need, the Lord Himself will send him, and you receive the help of man because the Lord helps you through man. But someone who is sent by God to help you will not oppress or abuse you. They will not exalt themselves in your life but the Lord. In fact their help will bring you closer to the Lord.

Therefore, never succumb to the wrong attitudes of man towards you because you fear to lose their help. If I mistreat you because I think that you need me I have missed the point. Focus on the Lord and on people who believe in you and inspire you to draw near to the Lord. Focus on the Lord and on the right people. Do not strive. Stay away from those that always seek what will profit only them at the expense of others.

You must know that you have a Father in heaven who watches over you and is in you. He knows the good and the bad about you but He still loves you with a steadfast and an everlasting love. In His mercy He spares and protects you from the evil you deserve and by His grace He gives the good you do not deserve. He knows the truth behind your smile and behind your tears. When no one believes in you He still believes in you. He is proud of you because of what He has invested in you. He sees the best He has put in you and He wants you to manifest the best of it. When people disappoint you He will never disappoint you. When they turn their back on you He is still ever present with you. When there is no one to rely on He is still a friend who is closer than a brother. When they disqualify you He qualifies you. He delivers you from all those who persecute you. He judges your cause and He is your defence. He is your refuge. He is a perfect Father and He wants you to be the best He created you to be. He wants you to shine so bright and show forth His light. He has good thoughts of you and He wants you to have a good future. He wants you to be well and to prosper in all you do. You are never alone because He is always with you. He is your teacher, your leader and your hero. He is everything to you and through Him you can do all things.

Vain is the Help of Man: (Psalm 108:12)

Psalm 108 was written by David the second and great king of Israel. The greatest secret of David was his trust and attitude towards the Lord. With total assurance David believed in enquiring from the Lord when he was faced with any challenge that was beyond his natural control.

He had the revelation that getting help from man without the help of God does not take you far and does not guarantee victory and success. The reason why king David would not go to ask for help from other kings to make his army strong against his opponents is because, he knew that human effort would not help him without God's help. He always chose to enquire from God and to get an instruction from God. If God said go and prosper he would go. If God said, "don't go", he would not go even if any king with a powerful army would offer to help him. The help of man without the help of God gets you nowhere.

Psalm 146:3, says, "Put not your trust in princes, nor in the son of man, in whom there is no help. His breath goeth forth, he returneth to his earth; in that very day his thoughts perish. Happy is he that hath the God of Jacob for his help, whose hope is in the Lord his God: which made heaven, and earth, the sea, and all that therein is; which keepeth truth for ever."

By saying don't put your trust in man we are simply saying, you find the right help only because God has given it to you or has made it available for you. That is to say the source of every effective help is God, whether it seems to come naturally or supernaturally. He is a God who knows everything before it happens and nothing escapes His control. To break down this further I would say, there are different levels of problems and different levels of solutions. Some solutions come through natural methods, and some can only come through the spirit of God/ through the anointing. Those who will help through natural methods and all those who will rely on the anointing of God to give solution are in the hand of God. We acknowledge the fact that God is the pivotal source of profitable help to man.

God is there in every level of our existence. He is not limited in the ways He can help us. We must not look up to man for help but up to God. Whenever somebody gives you help that impacts your life positively, it is because God is using them to help you. There is nothing a man has by himself. God has given us inherent wisdom in creation for us to be able function on earth. That is the wisdom of man and it is limited to the natural realm but it comes from God. God has given us potential, skills and abilities which are to help us in the fulfilment of the specific purposes we have on earth. All these potentials, kills, abilities and the inherent wisdom in us help us to fulfil our purposes. However, a man is only fully equipped to fulfil his purpose on earth after he has received Jesus and is filled with the His presence

When you see a man in the laboratory manufacturing a body lotion for people to use, you must not think that the wisdom to do so comes from man. God created the herbs and crops, and knew which ones will be processed for use by man and he gave man wisdom to do so. Psalm 104:14, says, "He causeth the grass to grow for the cattle, and herb for the service of man: that he may bring forth food out of the earth: and wine that maketh glad the heart of man and oil to make his face to shine, and bread which strengtheneth man's heart." Just because God has given the earth to man, does not mean He must not be acknowledged in the natural realm. He is still our source and the more we acknowledge Him is the more we see the manifestation of His glory in our lives.

When a prophet helps you through the power of God it is not just a man helping you with man's wisdom. A prophet is sought to solve problems that are above the natural methods of solutions. These are problems that have defeated the inherent wisdom and intelligence of man, and all the knowledge they have acquired. That is why a prophet does not use human efforts, ability, power, or wisdom to help; he uses God's power with God's counsel and his help goes beyond human efforts. So, a prophet is not made a prophet by human ability. God puts a mantle on him, which comes with an anointing and an angelic host to help him in his assignment and to fulfil his purpose. God gives anointing to His servants to help His people, and also to teach His people that there is nothing in life that is impossible with God. When the natural methods that we have devised through the wisdom of man fail, we find solution by allowing God to intervene through His Spirit.

In 2 kings 5:1, Naaman, a captain of the host of the king of Syria was sick with Leprosy, a sickness, not naturally curable through human effort. The king of Syria sent him with a letter to the king of Israel, to go and seek help from there, because there was a prophet there. The king of Israel said, "am I God, to kill and make alive, that this man doth send unto me to recover a man of his leprosy? Wherefore consider, I pray you and see how he seeketh a quarrel against me". So the king of Israel thought the king of Syria was seeking trouble with him. There are problems that kings can not solve and problems that great men can not solve. The prosperity of a nation does not come from kings or from great men. It comes from the Lord. When Elisha heard this he sent to the king, saying, "Why have you rent your clothes? Let him come now to me, and he shall know that there is a prophet in Israel." He said, he will know; that means he will become a witness of God because of the experience he will have with God. God can use a man but the solution comes from Him.

The Lord knows who to use to help us, whether in the natural way or supernatural. Ultimately even the natural is controlled by the supernatural even though the supernatural is often not acknowledged. The physical is birthed from the spiritual. The supernatural produces the natural. That means we do not put our trust in people in the natural but in the Lord. Any help that a man is able to give in the natural or supernatural manner, which profits us, is because he is given ability by God, to be profitable to others. This includes doctors, scientists and others.

So when we seek help our focus should be on God. Psalm 147:10, say, "He delighteth not in the strength of the horse: He taketh not pleasure in the legs of a man. The Lord taketh pleasure in them that fear Him, in those that hope in His mercy."

There is a Secret Place in God: (Psalm 91)

In order to dwell there, there are three necessary things required of you;
1.   Trust in the Lord's help with all your heart.
2.   God your hiding place (your refuge). Make Him your habitation.
3.   Set your love on God and seek to know Him more.

In His secret place you are protected and defended and you are not afraid of anything. No evil shall come upon you. His angels minister to you and help you. You walk in authority. By favour God elevates you. You see answers for your prayers. You are satisfied by long life and you see the salvation of the Lord.

God's Rest in Jesus:

For he that is entered into His rest, he also has ceased from his own works as did God.-Hebrews 4:10.

To enter into the rest of God is to receive His righteousness; to focus on His righteousness and to lean on it and not on our own. We are called to enter into His rest. We must rest our minds and souls in Him. To lean on/ focus on self righteousness is to be carnally minded. To be carnally minded is to mind the weakness of the flesh and to be carnally minded is death.-Romans 8:6. To be carnally minded is to carry the burden of your own labour (of the works of the flesh). One who has not entered into His rest finds it difficult to expect the perfect will of God to manifest. We are supposed to be spirit minded which is to focus on the finished work of Christ. We are called to cease from our own labour. That is the will of God and it is what enables us to manifest the glory of God. The glory of God is fulfilled when we by faith see the will of God fulfilled in our lives. Our labour now is to confess the Word of faith with boldness, because of Jesus.

Romans 8:1, Says, "There is therefore no condemnation to them which are in Christ Jesus, who walk not after flesh, but after the Spirit." Again in Romans 8:12, he says, "Therefore, brethren, we are debtors, not to the flesh, to live after the flesh." Firstly he shows us that it is not legal for anyone to condemn us if we are in Christ. Secondly he shows us that we do not owe the flesh to mind the things of the flesh. In Matthew 11:28, He says, "Come to me all ye that labour and heavy laden and I will give you rest. Take my yoke upon you, and learn of me; for I am meek and lowly in heart: and ye shall find rest unto your souls. For my yoke is easy and my burden is light" Here Jesus is talking to those who are labouring to obtain the righteousness of the law. Look at Jesus and rest in Him. Rest is found in Him. We are strong when we are resting in Jesus.

Hope:

Hope is one of the three most important things that Paul said we must pursue. The other two are faith and love, and love is the greatest. Hope is like a song that keeps a man who is on a journey to a specific place, on walking, in spite of the challenges on the road. When you know something great is coming though some things may seem to go wrong, with hope you do not give up because you know what is coming is coming for sure. When something is happening and it is not yet completed or fully fulfilled, with hope you know it shall be perfected and fulfilled for sure. Hope carries you to a place where your faith has allowed you to believe God for. Romans 5:3-5 says, "tribulation produces perseverance; and perseverance, character; and character, hope. Now hope does not disappoint, because the love of God has been poured out in our hearts by the Holy Spirit who was given to us. " It says hope does not disappoint because the love of God is shared abroad in our hearts. Meaning the love of God is the reason why we are full of hope. When you have hope no matter how bad things may seem you end up with the results you desire because you do not give up. Faith helps you to keep holding on to what you see inside. Hope helps you to keep doing what you have to do in order to see what you are expecting manifested. Because of

Jesus we have hope that whatever we trust God for according to His will, shall be manifested. Proverbs 10:28 says, "The hope of the righteous shall be gladness:"

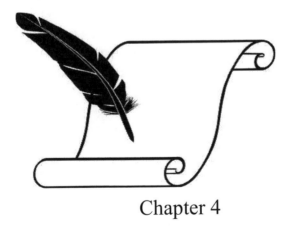

Chapter 4

THE KINGDOM OF GOD

The kingdom of God is the governance and rule of God, through which the will of God on earth is fulfilled and established. In Matthew 6:33, Jesus, said, "But seek ye first the kingdom of God and His righteousness." That means we have to seek the rule, the governance and the will of God. God rules on earth through His Word (His principles) and His Spirit. That means He reigns on earth through those who are filled with the knowledge of His Word and with His Spirit. His Word gives us His mind, His thoughts, His will and His principles. The Word of God builds us up to be like Christ. His Spirit teaches us, leads us and empowers us to manifest Christ, meaning to live and walk like Him. This is when the sons of God are manifesting. The church is in the kingdom of God and the kingdom of God is in the church.

What is found in the kingdom of God is everything that is found in love. Love rules in the kingdom of God. Anything that opposes love is not found in His kingdom. That is why the scripture says, "Seek first the kingdom of God and His righteousness." God is perfectly righteous because He is love. In Mark 12:28, one of the scribes once came to Jesus and asked, "Which is the first commandment. And Jesus answered him and said, the first commandment is, hear, o Israel; The Lord our God is one Lord: And though shalt love the Lord thy God with all thy heart, and with all thy soul, and with all thy mind, and with all thy strength: this is the first commandment. And the second is like, namely this, thou shalt love thy neighbour as thyself. There is none greater than these. And the scribe said unto Him, well, master, thou hast said the truth: for there is one God; and there is none other but he: And to love Him with all the heart, and with all the understanding, and with all the soul, and with all strength, and to love his neighbour as himself, is more than all whole burnt offerings and sacrifices. And when Jesus saw that He answered discreetly, he said unto him, thou art not far from the kingdom of God."

Luke 11:2 says, "And he said unto them, when ye pray, say, our Father which art in heaven, hallowed be thy name. Thy kingdom come, thy will be done on earth as it is in heaven." God wanted His kingdom to be established on earth so that His will be done on earth. He wants His will to be fulfilled on earth as it is in heaven. The will of God is what pleases Him. That simply means His will for the earth is so perfect. He wants it to be done on earths as it is in heaven; in heaven where satan has no place, no influence and no impact. That is the reason we must not ignore the power of God. Without the power of God we will never be able to fulfil the will God on earth as it is in heaven, unless you want to live out the will of satan on earth as it is in hell. .

Romans 14:17, says, "For the kingdom of God is not meat and drink; but righteousness, and peace, and joy in the Holy Ghost." That means where the kingdom of God is there will be peace, joy and righteousness. And that is what God wants us to pursue; His peace, His joy, and His righteousness. These three are fulfilled on earth for the profit of men and for the pleasure of God, when we allow Him to rule through His Word and His Spirit. That means it is not the will of God that people be filled with sorrow, and pain. God's desire is for the kingdom of God to be within us and for His will to be done in and through us. This is only made possible by the Word and the Spirit of God and for that purpose He has given us both these.

Everything we see happening on earth, through and in the lives of people has either one of the two sources; God or the devil. We live in a world which satan is seeking to control through his demonic forces, influences and works. John 10:10, says, "The thief cometh not, but for to steal, and to kill, and destroy:" If he is the thief it means he is not welcome. The thief is the enemy; He does not seek what is good for you. What he seeks for you today and tomorrow is only evil. But the good news is that Jesus said, in the same verse that, "I am come that they might have life and have it abundantly." Satan has endeavoured to plant as much seed of evil as possible in order to steal, to kill and to destroy lives of men on earth but Jesus came to give life in abundance. Jesus is doing the opposite. In Matthew 13:37 Jesus says to His disciples, "He that soweth the good seed is the Son of man; the field is the world: the good seed are the children of the kingdom; but the tares are the children of the wicked one; the enemy that soweth them is the devil;" In Luke 9:56, He says, "For the Son of man is not come to destroy men's lives, but to save men." Again He said, "every tree that my heavenly Father has not planted shall be up rooted". It is clear here that the only one who is pleased when lives are destroyed; when people are living in pain, in sorrow, and are not pleasing God, is satan.

Again in Luke 13:18-19, Jesus, said, "What is the kingdom of God like? What shall I compare it to? It is like a mustard seed, which a man took and planted in his garden. It grew, became a tree, and the birds of the air perched in its branches." Matthew 13:44, Jesus says, "Again, the kingdom of heaven is like unto treasure hid in a field; the which when a man hath found, he hideth, and for joy thereof goeth and selleth all that he hath and buyeth it. Verse 47, says, "Again the kingdom of heaven is like unto a net, that was cast into the sea, and gathered of every kind: which when it was full, they drew to shore, and sat down and gathered the good into vessels but cast the bad away." In summary all these verses are showing us the matchless worth and power of the kingdom of God. It is showing us how precious the kingdom of God is and how much impact it is able to make.

The primary key factor to the kingdom of God is faith. Faith comes from the Word of God and it opens the door for the Holy Spirit to work and flourish. No matter how much faith can be despised or taken lightly; it is the only precious currency in the spirit. It is what we need, in order to see all that the blood of Jesus has already purchased for us, manifest. Where there is faith, there the power of God will manifest. No wonder Paul said, "The kingdom of God is not a matter of talk, but of power."-1 Corinthians 4:20. Jesus said, "For this purpose the Son of God was manifested, that he might destroy the works of the devil." –1 John 3:8. The works of satan, which oppose the will of God, are destroyed through the power of God.

The kingdom of God is righteousness and peace and joy in the Holy Spirit – (Romans 14:17).

Righteousness:

Righteousness is right standing with God. It is a position of absolute and perfect obedience to the law of God; being perfectly pleasing to God. You are most likely thinking, "this is not possible for a man to achieve." Well, let us find out how this righteousness is fulfilled.

In Matthew 5:17, Jesus says, "Think not that I am come to destroy the law or the prophets: I am not come to destroy, but to fulfil." So Jesus is saying, I am not against the law or the prophets. He is on the same side with the law and the prophets. The law came from God and the prophets came from God. Their purpose was to show what pleases God and what does not please God. It was to show the will of God. The law was the standard given by God for man to live by. The prophets were the servants of God sent to get man to align with God according to the law. They persecuted many of them and killed some. So Jesus as the Son came with authority; as an heir and as the owner. That is why the scripture says, "He came unto his own and His own received Him not."-John 1:11. This is what the parable depicts when Jesus spoke of a man who planted a vine yard and committed it to the husband men. He says when the man sent his servants to husbandmen to get fruits they killed them one after another. Then he sent his son thinking they will respect him but they killed him as well.-Matthew 21:33-39.

Jesus pointed out in Matthew 5:17 that He came to fulfil the law. He did not come to teach it harder or better but to fulfil it. In verse 18 He says, "For verily I say unto you, till heaven and earth pass, one jot or one title shall in no wise pass from the law, till it be fulfilled." He is not saying there is a chance that it will be fulfilled. He is saying it will surely be fulfilled. That means the law was predestined to be fulfilled. The question is who will fulfil it and how? In verse 20 He says, "For I say unto you, that except your righteousness exceed the righteousness of the scribes and Pharisees, ye shall in no case enter into the kingdom of heaven."

The scribes and the Pharisees are people who were well taught and trained in the law. They studied it well; and they knew the benefits of obedience and consequences of disobedience to the law. They spent years trying to attain perfection through obedience of the law but they failed because of the inherent nature of sin in the flesh. All that effort is what Paul counted as nothing so that He could attain the righteousness of Jesus. Jesus is the one who fulfilled the law. The law is perfect but Jesus was perfect even before the perfect law was given to man. The law came from Him and He came and fully obeyed His own law to man perfectly. He first fulfilled it by obeying it perfectly. He obeyed the law not only outwardly but inwardly. He was not only perfect through outward performance but in the heart as well. So we are not called to lean on the righteousness of our obedience to the law but to lean on the righteousness of His perfect obedience to the law.

Jesus did not condemn anyone for not being in absolute and perfect obedience to the law, not even His disciples. His greatest desire was that they might believe with all their hearts in Him who fully obeyed all the law. When a woman was brought for Jesus to judge her for she was caught in adultery He did not judge her according to the law. Even if she never committed adultery she will be condemned if He judged her. According to the law she had to die, but He said, I do not condemn you, go and sin no more. Simply put He was saying, go and do what is good according to the law, knowing that your justification does not come from your own obedience to the law, because that is impossible. Jesus is the only one who perfectly honoured and obeyed God on earth. When we align with Him by faith His righteousness is imputed on us by grace. He becomes our righteousness and we become the righteousness of God. When He says unless your righteousness exceed that of the scribes and Pharisees you can not enter the kingdom of heaven, it means you can not enter through your own efforts to obey the law. That is what the scribes and Pharisees were doing; labouring to be perfect according to the law. They were not wrong in seeking to obey the law, but in rejecting the only one who had all power to obey it perfectly, and who was the door for man to perfect righteousness. That is why in Matthew 21:42, He says, "Did ye never read in the scriptures, the stone which the builders rejected, the same has become the head of the corner: this is the Lord's doing, and it is marvellous in our eyes?" So we are suppose to teach people not to honour the law. The law is good and perfect. But we are suppose to help them understand that they are not justified, saved and perfected through their own effort. This is what Jesus did to the woman, when He said, "neither do I condemn you, go and sin no more."

Those upon whom the righteousness of Jesus is imputed by faith are also qualified by Him to see in their lives everything God promised to those that will fully obey the law. In this way as Jesus said, what was spoken concerning the law is fulfilled. When we receive Jesus through faith He comes inside of us and we understand when we are taught correctly that there is no more condemnation for us. In Him we are also empowered by the Holy Spirit to pursue the will of God passionately and with the knowledge of Him. We have the nature of God flowing in us through the Holy Spirit. So we don't find ourselves miserably trying to obey commandments that are burdensome. We are lead by His Spirit and we rejoice in seen His righteousness.

Colossians 2:13 says, "And you being dead in your sins and the uncircumcision of your flesh hath he quickened together with Him, having forgiven you all trespasses; Blotting out the handwriting of ordinances that was against us, which was contrary to us, and took it out of the way, nailing it on the cross." The law worked against man on earth because it made sin more sinful and because of it they knew sin and died to the Lord. It was contrary to man because of the nature and the weakness of man's flesh. So the ordinance of the righteousness of works made it impossible for man to be able stand in the presence of God. It disqualified man because of His nature. But the verse above says, Jesus took it out of the away and nailed it on the cross, by paying the price for man's weakness and sin in advance. It stood in the way of man but Jesus took it away. Therefore, the judgement and condemnation of one by another has been abolished. God's forgiveness means God separating man from his sin and the sinful nature of his flesh. But above all, those who are born of God do not owe the flesh or satan anything. They have died to sin and to the world, and they live in Christ. They have put off the body of sin. They have passed completely from death to life.

Peace:

Jesus is the Prince of peace (Isaiah 9:6). Where He reigns there His peace is. He gives us supernatural peace concerning the past, the now and the future. His peace is the result of the freedom He gives. It is the kind of peace that no one else and nothing on earth can give. In Him we rest our minds and souls. Wherever He enters peace enters. That is why He said to His disciples, "when you enter a house salute it, and if the house be worthy let your peace come upon it: but if it be not worthy, let your peace return to you."-Matthew 10:12-13. In Him we have peace that a natural man can not understand.

To His disciples Jesus said, "Peace I leave with you, my peace I give unto you: not as the world giveth, give I unto you. Let not your heart be troubled, neither let it be afraid.-John 14:27. Where there is fear there is no peace because fear involves torment. But the love of Jesus casts out all fear from us. Because of Jesus we have peace in God and peace with God. That is why in John 14:27, He says also, "neither it be afraid." Peace is the absence of fear, worry and trouble in the heart and mind, in spite of what might be happening around. Jesus doesn't want you to worry, to fear or to be troubled.

In Philippians 4:6 He says, "Be careful for nothing; but in everything by prayer and supplication with thanksgiving let your requests be made known unto God. And the peace of God, which passeth all understanding, shall keep your hearts and minds through Christ Jesus." What this really means is let nothing cause you to fear, to worry or to be troubled, but present your desires to the Lord in prayer and you will receive supernatural peace from Him. The peace of God is for our hearts and minds. When your heart and mind are without peace your faith becomes weak. In 1 Timothy 6:10, Paul says, "For the love of money is the root of all evil: which while some coveted after, they have erred from the faith, and pierced themselves through with many sorrows."

Joy:

Psalm 16:11 says, "In Your presence there is fullness of joy." Those who are born of God have been born into His joy. The spirit of God fills us with joy. We are suppose to praise and worship Him with joy always and to serve Him with gladness. His joy is our strength even in adversity because in Him we rejoice always hoping for His glory. We rejoice because He has given us the power to be called the children of God and He has made us heirs. We rejoice knowing that through Him we have victory in all things. Everything the Holy Spirit whispers in us produces joy in us. The voice of Jesus produces in us joy. In John 3:29 John the Baptist says, "He that hath the bride is the bride groom: but the friend of the bridegroom, which standeth and heareth Him, rejoiceth greatly because of the bridegroom's voice: this my joy therefore is fulfilled." His voice comforts us and removes all sorrow from our hearts.

To the Philippians 3:1 Paul said, "Finally, brethren, rejoice in the Lord." Here Paul was not encouraging them to rejoice for a moment or over something specific. He was counselling them to continually rejoice in the Lord. It means whether things seem good or not, whether people love or hate you, whether they accept or reject you, whether things seem to go according to your plans or not. We rejoice because of the joy of the Lord and because His kingdom is peace, joy and righteousness in the Holy Ghost.

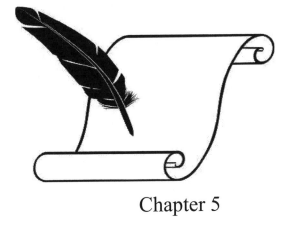

Chapter 5

THE HOLY SPIRIT

The Holy Spirit is the Spirit of God. He is the dwelling place of those who belong to Christ and He also dwells in them. Paul in Romans 8:9, said, "But you are not in the flesh, but in the Spirit, if so be that the Spirit of God dwells in you. " This implies that once you are born again you come live in God's Spirit though you still have a physical body and are on earth. That is why Hebrews 12:22- 25 says, "But ye are come unto mount Sion, and unto the city of the living God, the heavenly Jerusalem, and to an innumerable company of angels, To the general assembly and church of the firstborn, which are written in heaven, and to God the Judge of all, and to the spirits of just men made perfect, And to Jesus the mediator of the new covenant, and to the blood of sprinkling, that speaketh better things than that of Abel." Paul to the Romans said, "For the kingdom of God is not eating and drinking, but righteousness and peace and joy in the Holy Ghost."-(Romans 14:17). Once we come into the kingdom of God we are in His Spirit and His presence in us.

God does everything He does in our lives through the Holy Spirit. The Spirit is the one who brings to pass what God has spoken over us. In Zachariah 4:6, the angel said, "This is the word of the Lord unto Zerubbabel, saying, not by might, nor by power, but by my Spirit, saith the Lord of hosts. Who art thou, o great mountain? Before Zerubbabel thou shall become a plain:" That means the will of God does not happen by any other power or might but by the power of the Holy Spirit. He is also like an invisible man who is always with and in those who belong to Christ and is present everywhere. This means He is a person with a personality and a character.

John 16:13, says, "He will lead you into all truth." He leads us into all truth and He shows us things to come. In Him are the thoughts of God concerning the past, the now and the future. In Him is all knowledge. Luke 2:25, says, "And, behold, there was a man in Jerusalem, whose name was Simeon; and the same man was just and devout, waiting for the consolation of Israel: and the Holy Ghost was upon him. And it was revealed to him by the Holy Ghost, that he should not see death, before he had seen the Lord's Christ. And he came by the Spirit into the temple: and when the parents brought in the child Jesus, to do for him after the custom of the law,"

The first important thing we hear about this man (Simeon) is that the Holy Spirit was upon him. Everything else that was mentioned in the verses below was possible because the Holy Spirit was upon this man. The second thing is that he had a revelation concerning Jesus by the Holy Spirit. And the third thing is that he came by the Spirit into the temple. That means he was lead to go to the temple by the Holy Spirit on the day that Jesus was brought for dedication.

In Luke 2:30, Simeon says, "For mine eyes have seen thy salvation, which thou hast prepared before the face of all people; A light to the Gentiles, and the glory of thy people Israel. And Joseph and His mother marvelled at those things that were spoken of Him." In this verse Simeon is sharing the glorious revelation that God through the Holy Spirit has given Him concerning Jesus. So the Holy Spirit confirmed to him that that specific child was the messiah; the one bringing salvation of people. The things this man said by the Holy Spirit amazed even the parents of this child. This tells me that the things that God has prepared to be fulfilled through our lives exceed what our parents, friends and people who know us can imagine. This means that it is important for us to be in tune/ in sync with the Holy Spirit.

Jesus in acts 1:8, said to His disciples, "But ye shall receive power after that the Holy Spirit has come upon you." That means, once the Holy Spirit comes upon us we receive the power of God. It is through the power of the Holy Spirit that we are able execute the will of God and fulfil our mandate on earth as the church. He gives us gifts and abilities that enable us to serve God without being confined/ restricted to human limitations. It is through the Holy Spirit that Moses performed signs and wonders in Egypt and was able to lead the children of Israel out of Egypt. By the power of the Holy Spirit David killed Goliath; Daniel was ten times wiser than the magicians; the sea parted before the Israelites; Shadrack, Meshack and Abednego were not burnt in the furnace of fire; Jesus walked on water; the dead were raised. How? The how belongs to the Holy Spirit.

When Mary the mother of Jesus was told that she would conceive and give birth to a child, she asked how it would be. The angel said to her, "The Holy Ghost shall come upon you and the power of the most high shall overshadow you."- Luke 1:35. Everything that God has predestined to happen in our lives, for our assignments, purposes and destinies will happen by the power of the Holy Spirit.

To us who believe in Jesus, it is said that the Holy Spirit is our comforter. - John 16:7. He comforts and strengthens us and helps us to remain focused on the purpose. He renews and refreshes us inside. He strengthens us against any affliction or resistance on the out side. He strengthens us to continue pursuing what God has set before us. Jesus has promised us that He would not leave us alone, but with the Holy Spirit. That means the Holy Spirit is here for us. Can you imagine what it means to understand that the Holy Spirit is here for you? We do everything in Him and with Him. He is our secret place which is hidden from the world. He is our best friend and he wants to be our friend every day. When you are broken, down and weak He is there as a friend who cares to strengthen you.

One of the greatest promises that God made to the church was that He would send the Holy Spirit. And indeed the Holy Spirit is here and indeed the church is not its own. Jesus Himself is the one who baptises us with the Holy Spirit. In John in 1:33, John the Baptist says, "And I knew Him not: but He that sent me to baptise with water, the same said unto me, upon whom thou shalt see the Spirit descending, and remaining on Him, the same is He which baptizeth with the Holy Ghost." This is the testimony of the Father.

The best we can do for our relationship with the Holy Spirit is to fellowship with Him, by spending time with Him and obeying Him. It is a powerful thing just to spend time praising God, worshipping Him, listening to Him and talking to Him concerning what is in our hearts. We can also cultivate our relationship with the Holy Spirit by praying in the spirit. The more we do this is the more we grow in faith and the more we draw close to God.

The more we fellowship with Holy Spirit is the more He reveals to us the treasures/ riches in Christ. By riches I am not referring to material possessions, but things far greater than anything material. Ephesians 3:8, says, "To me, who am less than the least of all the saints, this grace was given, that I should" preach among the Gentiles the unsearchable riches of Christ," He calls them unsearchable riches. You can not find them out except by the Spirit of God. Ephesians 3:14-16, says, "For this reason I bow my knees to the Father of our Lord Jesus Christ, from whom the whole family in heaven and earth is named, that He would grant you, according to the riches of His glory, to be strengthened with might through His Spirit in the inner man,"

The riches of His glory are the riches that come with His presence. This refers to the mysteries of His wisdom, love and power in Christ, which are revealed to us by His Spirit. 1 Corinthians 2:7-10, says, "But we speak the wisdom of God in a mystery, the hidden *wisdom* which God ordained before the ages for our glory, which none of the rulers of this age knew; for had they known, they would not have crucified the Lord of glory. But as it is written: "Eye has not seen, nor ear heard, Nor have entered into the heart of man. The things which God has prepared for those who love Him." But God has revealed *them to* us through His Spirit. For the Spirit searches all things, yes, the deep things of God."

Colossians 1:2-4, says, " that their hearts may be encouraged, being knit together in love, and *attaining* to all riches of the full assurance of understanding, to the knowledge of the mystery of God, both of the Father and of Christ, in whom are hidden all the treasures of wisdom and knowledge." This verse proves that these treasures are the treasure and riches of understanding, of knowledge and of wisdom. He speaks of the full assurance of understanding, to the acknowledgement of God (that is the mystery of the power and greatness of the God-head), and of the Father (the mystery of the Love of the Father) and of Christ (the mystery of the Son of God who is wisdom in us). A mystery is the truth that can only be known by revelation of the Spirit.

The gifts of the Holy Spirit:

God works in us and through us by the Holy Spirit. To be filled by God Spirit and Power, is something we must desire with everything in us. We must love and treasure the Holy Spirit as our best friend. But we must understand that the Holy is here on earth on a mission. He is sent on a mission. He is not here with His own agenda but he is here with a mission given to Him by Jesus. He is sent for the church, to equip the church and help the church in its mandate. Therefore we can not do without Him. We can not win without Him. We need Him more every day. We must cleave to Him. 1Corinthians 2:10..., says, He searches the deep things of God. The church was instructed by Jesus to wait in Jerusalem until the promise of the Father was fulfilled. And they waited until this promise was fulfilled on the day of Pentecost.

 2 Timothy 1:7 says, "God has not given us the spirit of fear, but of love, power and sound mind." Those are the three things the church needs in order to effectively be the salt of the world. To be the salt of the world speaks of the impact of our influence. Love, power and sound mind are indispensable if he church is to impact the world. We are

empowered by the Spirit of God to manifest the love, the power and the wisdom of God on earth.

The Holy Spirit gives the church abilities that elevate it in its operation to a level above that of a mere human being. Without the abilities given by the Holy Spirit the church will be limited in its impact and in the fulfilment of its purpose. There is so much God has to reveal to us, in us and through us by His Spirit; more than we have seen. Because of this, we are instructed by Paul in 1 Corinthians 14:1, to desire spiritual gifts. In 1 Corinthians 12:8, Paul gives us a list of nine gifts of the Holy Spirit. He says, "For to one is given by the Spirit the word of wisdom; to another the word of knowledge by the same Spirit: To another faith by the same Spirit; to another the gifts of healing by the same Spirit; to another the working of miracle; to another prophecy; to another discerning of Spirits; to another diverse tongues; to another interpretation of tongues: But all these worketh that one and selfsame Spirit, dividing to every man severally as He will." What we are seeing here is that all these gifts are given by one Spirit; they are from one Spirit. They also flow by one Spirit. That means there is unity and harmony among all these gifts. They cohesively work to fulfil the will of God. It is the Holy Spirit working in all these gifts.

All these gifts are important and are given for edification of the church. In 1 Corinthians 14:26,

Paul says, "How is it then, brethren? When ye come together, every one of you hath a psalm, hath a doctrine, hath a tongue, hath a revelation, hath an interpretation. Let all be done unto edifying." I would also say that the gifts of the Spirit show forth God's might and power.

Revelatory Gifts:

1.   The gift of the word of wisdom gives one ability to solve problems with a very high level of divine wisdom. This is where a person is given divine ability to know what to say, what to do and what choice to make in order to address a certain matter or solve a certain problem. We see this gift manifest through men like Solomon, Joseph, Elihu and many others. When two women were brought before Solomon fighting over a child he knew exactly what say in order to solve the problem. We know God gave Joseph wisdom to provide solution to a future problem that God revealed to Pharaoh in dreams. When Job was confused by what was happening in his life and his three friends had run out of what to say to answer to Job, Elihu knew exactly what to say and it worked.

2.   The gift of the Word of knowledge gives a person ability to know things he would not naturally know unless he is told. This can be past or present information about someone or something. This is when God spiritually gives a man

information he does not have. Through the word of knowledge Peter knew that Ananias and Sapphira were not telling the truth when they said they brought all the money from the sales of their possessions.-Acts 5:1-9. Through this gift a man's spiritual eyes are open and he can see things that have happened or are happening while he was or is not there.

3.   The gift of discerning of spirits, gives a man divine ability to know when someone is carrying a contrary spirit. The spirit of God makes the spirit of a man to be sensitive in the spirit realm. There was a woman who followed Paul and company as they went to prayer. She was possessed with a spirit of divination and through it she brought her masters much gain through soothsaying. She followed them crying out saying, "These men are the servants of the most high God, which shew unto us the way of salvation. And Paul being grieved, turned and said to the spirit, I command thee in the name of Jesus Christ to come out of her,"-Acts 16:17-18. Paul was sensitive in the spirit that he was able to know that she was not saying what she was saying by the Spirit of God.

Power Gifts:

1.   The gift of faith gives a man ability to believe God for things that even believers find too hard to believe God for. This is ability to believe

beyond every limit. This is faith that makes the hardest matters seem so easy. In 2 Kings 3:17, Elisha says, "For thus saith the Lord, ye shall see no rain; yet that valley shall be filled with water, that ye may drink, both ye, and your cattle, and your beasts." But then he adds and say, "And this is but a light thing in the sight of the Lord:"-2 kings 3:18. Joshua 10:12-13 says, "Then spake Joshua to the Lord in the day when the Lord delivered up the amorites before the children of Israel, and he said in the sight of Israel, Sun stand still upon Gibeon; and thou, moon, in the alley of Ajalon. So the Sun stood still, and the moon stopped, till the nation avenged itself on its enemies," How did even the thought cross his mind to do that? Who told him that he had power to do that? These people are always ready to believe God even for what is called impossible, but to them nothing is impossible.

2.   The gifts of healings give a man ability to heal all kinds of diseases and sicknesses through the anointing of the Holy Spirit. People with these gifts have anointing to heal the human soul and body. There is no kind of sicknesses whether in the blood, or deformation in the bones, or any wrong in the flesh that they can not cast out. They have by grace a revelation that enables them to destroy sickness whether it is mastered or understood by man or not. It does not matter how bad the disease is and at what state is the sickness of the person.

They heal a person who is almost dying of sickness as if it is just a minor issue. There were ten lepers one time, who saw Jesus passing and cried out saying, "Jesus, Master, have mercy on us!" All that Jesus said to these men was go show yourself to the priests and on the way these men were healed. - Luke 17:11-14. People who have the gift of healings are not moved to fear by any disease or the condition of the one who is sick. They believe in the healing power of Jesus. They know that healing has already been made legal and has been given by the stripes of Jesus. They understand that Jesus has already suffered stripes that people may not suffer because of sickness. They know the will of God and that only satan is happy when sickness is killing people. They believe in the healing anointing and for them the healing anointing is stronger than any sickness. They believe that God's anointing can fix every wrong in the human body.

3.   The gift of working of miracles gives a man ability to do things that are considered impossible for a human being to do. Miracles are acts that a man has no ability to do naturally. These are acts that defy human nature and are not possible through human ability. Through this gift a man is able to defy the laws of nature. It was a miracle when Jesus walked on water, because he defied the law of gravity and was able to walk on water without sinking.-Matthew 14:26. It was a miracle

when Elisha caused an axe head to float on water.-2 kings 6:6. It was a miracle when Jesus sent Peter to go and get money from the mouth of a fish. In order to see a miracle they forgot the human limitations and saw only God doing what they wanted to see. Miracles are possible when a man taps into the authority of God's ability. When you get to this level nothing is impossible and no problem is a serious issue.

Gifts of Utterance:

1.   The gift of prophecy gives one ability to know things that are going to happen in future. This is ability to see clearly and know with certainty events before they happen. Through the prophetic gift the Spirit of God gives direction and comfort to the church concerning the future. Through the prophetic gift a man is able with knowledge of truth to declare and enforce the will of God concerning the present and the future.

2.   The gift of diverse kinds of tongues gives a man ability to communicate a message from the Lord to the people, in tongues. This gift is effective and profitable to the church with help of the gift of the interpretation of tongues.

3.   The gift of the interpretation of tongues is ability given to a person to know the meaning of words spoken in the tongues and to give interpretation of the message thereof.

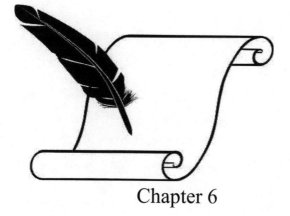

Chapter 6

PASSING THE TEST:

Every test of heart and character in life culminates with an experience that seems unfair and often shameful and putting someone very low in life. This is not a permanent stay, but just a temporal state. Jesus went through the same, Joseph went through the same, David went through the same, Job went through the same and Modecai went through the same. In order to pass the test you need humility; stay put and don't be anxious. Without humility we would be very anxious. Without humility you would give up.

I want to share a few things from the life of Joseph, David, Job and Modecai's, concerning the unique challenges they faced and how they overcame.

What was unique about Joseph's situation was that it seemed as if his main enemies were his own family. It seemed as if those who were the root cause of this trial of many years of his life were his own brothers. They took away from him the opportunity to grow with his parents. They took away from him the love and support of family. He was out there as a slave and had to just survive with this memory of the cruelty of his brothers. It seemed as if he was brought so low in life, in spite of how much potential and intelligence he had, simply because of the jealousy of his brothers. It seemed as if there was no hope for him to have any good future. For any man anywhere in the world, that would be a very painful situation. What I respect about him is that all those facts and realities did not corrupt him from the love of God. He still loved God and he still honoured God. It took uncommon humility to face that situation and win. In the end God gave Joseph wisdom to understand that all that happened to him was part of the plan. And Joseph said to his brothers, "Now therefore be not grieved, nor angry with yourselves, that ye sold me hither: for God did send me before you to preserve life." It took a lot of humility for this man to go through all of this and remain focused on God until God elevated him.

As for David what he faced was a very tricky situation. David himself believed in honouring God and in honouring the anointing of the Spirit of God. Because of envy and jealousy he was persecuted by a man who was once anointed by God to be king. The situation David faced was that he was persecuted by a man he believed in honouring especially because of the anointing. He was not honouring this man by force but it was his faith and also because he loved God and he loved to be aligned with God. The same man was seeking to kill him without a cause. This man was the source of pain and confusion for David. So what David did was to run for his life but he never stopped honouring this man. So David ran because he had no choice. To fight back would be to stand against his own faith, so all he could do was to go into hiding for his own protection. I honour this about him because in spite of this situation he still chose to align with God all the way. Even when Saul who sought his life was finally killed, David did not honour the man who killed him, but was displeased with him. He did not stop honouring Saul even when Saul who wanted to kill him was dead. This reminds of me Cindy Trimm saying, "Spiritual protocol is not temporal but spiritual."

Job was a man whom God allowed satan to try in the worst way you can imagine. He faced evil in every area of his life. At that very low state of his life his three friends started addressing him and commenting without understanding of his situation. They accused and condemned him because they lacked understanding and knowledge of what to say. So in stead of strengthening and supporting Job they became the very people that pulled him down. They did not treat him with mercy and love. I respect Job not only for having the capacity to endure that, but also for his courage to resist and refuse their accusations and condemnation against him. I also honour Elihu for his wisdom to reveal the righteousness of God to Job and to the three friends of Job, instead of focusing on the righteousness of job.

Modecai was a man of faith. He saw beyond his current experiences. He was able to couch Esther towards the destiny that God had prepared for her. He couched her as if he was sure that she would be chosen from among all the princesses to be the queen. She was not even a princess by birth but he believed in her. People of faith believe in other people's potentials. There was a man who was very close to the king and was loved by the king. This man, Haman, undermined Modecai and hated him. He hated him especially because Modecai refused to bow to him. Modecai refused to bow to Haman and Haman was offended by that. A wise man and a man of faith will always reject and oppose oppression. A wise man and a man of faith will always refuse to worship a man. Modecai was courageous enough to refuse to bow to Haman. He made the choice not to bow while everyone else, including all of the king's servants at the gate, was bowing. It was actually the king's command that everyone must bow and reverence Haman at the king's gate. Mordecai did not fear Haman nor the king's command in this regard. Those who fear man in stead of fearing God bow to man in stead of bowing to God. While all this was happening Modecai was just spending his time seating at the king's gate. He was not a man known or honoured by the king or any other man. But he did not base his attitude and choices on his title or position in society. He was a man of courage.

What I learn from all these men is that humility is what helps someone to remain aligned with God even at the lowest point of life, and to follow God to the place of promotion/ elevation and of destiny. I also realised that it is important to have courage and strength (faith) in order to win in life.

It is important to know in life that God does not use what He has not tested. Before He makes you shine He will take you through the fire. Before He elevates you He will hide you, when He is processing you. That is because if you be exposed prematurely, you may miss the mark in fulfilling your purpose. When God speaks a special word over your life, gives you anointing and shows you more it is not just for you. It is for those He will use you to bless, for His name's sake.

Overcoming Negative Emotions when Making Decisions:

Do not ever in life make decisions to favour your emotions. Make decisions to favour the perfect will of God for your life. Decisions made based on emotions can lead someone out of the path to their destiny. Peter, most likely because of emotions could not accept that Jesus was going to die as He foretold. But Jesus looked at Peter, and said, "Get thee behind me satan; for thou savourest not the things that be of God but those that be of man."- Matthew 16:23. Peter did not understand that the assignment of Jesus was bigger than just spending time with them and going around preaching and healing people. This is the problem we find sometimes in families. They fail to understand that we are not born in our families just to be with our families, live for our families, to please our families, to serve our families, do everything for our families and to succeed for our families. It is not just about our families. That is why Jesus said, you seek not the things that are of God but of man. Things of man are things that please man and puts man at comfort, but do not please God. That means through our emotions satan can get access to manipulate us to oppose the will of God. If ever anyone will, through emotions, speak against the will of God for your destiny, you must do what Jesus did. You must rebuke satan and reject their words. Give satan no room.

Our assignments go far beyond our families. So the sacrifices we have to make must not be looked at as unfair realities. The perfect will of God for you is to see you fulfil the original purpose and plan of God for your life. Your emotions have a voice, but your faith sees far beyond your emotions. If you have made some mistakes in the past forgive yourself and move on. Don't let your past mistakes captivate your life and destiny. If you have incurred some consequences that are and will continue to impact your life, it is a fact that they are a part of your life. But it is time for you to mix the facts with wisdom and make the right choices that will cause you to live a life that gives God glory. The greatest tragedy in a man's life is not that he has made some mistakes. The greatest tragedy is if the plan of God for his life never gets fulfilled because he is stuck in the past. Break every emotional stronghold from past mistakes and experiences. Your faith is your response to the navigation system of God that leads you through the path of the plan of God for your life. Faith leads you to the solution. Guilt and negative emotions have a way of leading you to back mistakes again. Say yes to God and follow Him.

He knows the best. He is waiting for you in the future, not in the past. There is no kind of mistake or wrong that does not dissolve in the eyes of God's love, when it is acknowledged.

The Burden of the Mind versus the Burden of the Spirit:

Many times we have heard it said that if there are situations in our lives that are beyond our control, we must put them in the hands of God. And some of us would pray and say, "Lord, this, I leave in your hands". But straight after that the person who just prayed that prayer still spends time worrying and agonising over the same situation. Ultimately that leaves their minds burdened with worries and thoughts of fear, uncertainty and doubts. They carry these burdens in their minds wherever they go and no matter what they do.

It is absolutely not the will of God and it is not of God that we carry such burdens in our minds. Anyone who is burdened in their mind, because of situations, will find it difficult to conceive good things in the spirit or to birth the good they have conceived. Such burdens only help them to miscarry what they have conceived in the spirit. Spiritual pregnancy is a spiritual burden which is the result of something you have conceived in the spirit and must be birthed through prayer, followed by the necessary action steps.

If you have effectively given your burdens to the Lord you should not continue struggling with anxiety, worry and stress over the same thing you have given to the Lord. But how can one ensure this? Proverbs 24:10 says, "If you faint on the day of adversity then your strength is small." That means you need strength in order to win on the day of adversity. Daniel 11:32 Says, "The people that know their God shall be strong and do great exploits"

Many of us on earth define our lives based on our experiences with people and with our physical environments. We are conscious of our experiences with our parents, siblings, friends, colleagues, fellow Christians and so on. But we have every little or no consciousness of true experiences with God. We are often conscious of how unfaithful people can be but not conscious of how faithful God is.

This is the reason why the Holy Spirit saw it fit to differentiate between man and God. Numbers 23:19 says, "God is not a man that He may lie, nor a son of man that He might repent." The promises of God are faithful and are without error. The word of God and the promises of God do not proceed from a weak God but from a powerful and mighty God who is without error.

Once you have committed any situation in the hand of God, you need to focus on the solution, with an expectation. Give thanks for what you are hoping for, as if it has already happened. Prepare to walk in it. Invest more of the word of God in yourself.

Strength and Courage:

A person who walks on earth with strength and courage will be able to fulfil what God has set for him/ her to fulfil without fear. Such a person will be able to overcome every obstacle on the way and will surely do great exploits.

Be strong: Don't be shaken, don't waver, don't stagger at the promises of God and do not doubt. Be firm at your stand on the word of God. This is possible if you build yourself up by the word of God and if you meditate on it. Find strength in the Love of God.

Be courageous: Take a stand and make a move without hesitating or looking left or right. Focus on the results and make a move. Be confident in God and act seeing the results in your mind. Make a move without fear. Let nothing stop you from making a move. Courage is what empowers you to make the necessary move. Act without being afraid of anyone or anything. Let not panic fill your bones. Let the fire of the Holy Ghost fill up your bones.

With strength and courage we must follow the righteousness of God diligently, and do not turn to the left or right. In other words we must have strength and courage to execute God's righteousness and justice, and not be intimidated by any adversary. The majority of people on earth, including those who go to church do not honour God's righteousness. They judge according to their opinions and oppress whoever does not have anything or potential to profit them.

There are people here on earth that will only see the importance and the beauty of the righteousness of God when they see us manifest it; when they see the justice of God manifesting through us. There are people who through us will learn to fear the Lord. That's why nothing we do should be about us but about Him.

Seeing as God sees:

In Samuel 16:7, the Lord said to Samuel, concerning Eliab, "Look not on his countenance, or on the height of stature, because I have refused him; for the Lord seeth not as man seeth; for man looketh on the outward appearance but God looks at the heart, not at the outward appearance." Many people today accept people because of what they have on the outside, rather than what they have on the inside. They respect the possessions the person has on the outside than what is in his heart. Based on this they reject who God has accepted and accept one whose heart is not right before God. We must not be moved by houses, cars and money and let them influence our attitudes towards people. We must look at all people through the eyes of God. That way we will not be deceived.

Samuel was a man of God with a good heart and he was just trying to find the man the Lord wanted him to anointing king. But Samuel at first was focusing on what he was seeing on the outside. God is not looking for people who are perfect on the outside. He is looking for people that are after His heart; people that sincerely love and fear/ honour Him; people that love His righteousness and justice.

Sometimes people fail to move on peacefully after they have been rejected because they think they have lost something great which those who rejected them had. Often it is because they are so focused on the perfection that is outward and not inward. In 1 Samuel 16:1, God said to Samuel, "How long wilt thou mourn for Saul, seeing I have rejected him from reigning over Israel?" Sometimes we carry on mourning over people and things that God is removing and killing from our lives and destinies. In 1 Samuel 16:2, God said to Samuel, "Fill thine horn with oil, and go, I will send thee to Jesse the Bethlehemite: for I have provided me a king among his sons." Only God sees the best.

Carrying your Own Cross:

Matthew 16:21-24 says, "From that time forth began Jesus to show unto His disciples how that He must go to Jerusalem and suffer many things of the elders and chief priests and scribes and be killed and be raised again the third day. Then Peter took him and began to rebuke him saying, be it far from thee, Lord: this shall not be unto thee. But He turned and said unto Peter; get thee behind me, satan: thou art an offence unto me; for thou savourest not the things that be of God, but those that be of men. And then said Jesus unto his disciples, if any man will come after me, let him deny himself, and take up his cross and follow me." What does carrying your own cross mean? The cross is a place of crucifixion, a place of denying your own will, a place of dying to yourself (letting go of vain glory which is to be seen or known by people). It is a place of great humility where you seem to lose something more precious to you for Christ. It was on the cross that Jesus said, My God my God, why have you forsaken me.

What happens at the Cross?

• People put on you the banner of accusations, just like Jesus had an inscription of accusation above his head on the cross. It was written, "King of Jews". What they say thinking their taking you down will become the thing that will lift you up.

• Enduring the pain and shame with those who have no regard for God. The scripture says Jesus was numbered with the transgressors.- Isaiah 53:12. It is as if the portion of the wicked has become your portion.

• You are challenged and mocked by men.

• Your potential and gifts from God are undermined by men.

• There seems to be darkness all around and some times you are not sure what to do.

• It seems as thou God has forsaken you.

• Your prayer is undermined by men. They think you are praying in vain.

The most important thing is that you go through all these for Jesus. The cross is the bridge you go through to a place of distinguished elevation. This is a process through which your heart is tested and your attitude is groomed. In the process you go through a number of defining moments where you are thoroughly prepared for elevation, to serve God in a uniquely high level. You are brought to a place of complete sincerity and authenticity. The assignment that you are prepared for is your passion but the cross is not pleasant at all. It involves pain and sorrow and rejection.

When people see something unpleasant happening to someone they want to master what's happening and to understand why. Now it makes sense if brothers and sisters in the Lord will do so because they desire to help. But if the same people turn into accusers in the process, something is wrong. When they fail to understand what is happening they turn to judge and condemn. Sometimes they do so backing themselves up with scriptures, just as the friends of Job did. The truth is, it does not take strength, wisdom or greatness to persecute someone who is down. Job said to his friends, you be saying to yourselves, "Why persecute we him seen the root of the matter is found in him."-Job 19:28. You must not allow yourself the time and luxury to mind those who are accusing you and concluding things against you without knowledge.

Chapter 7

UNFEIGNED FAITH

Hebrews 11:6, says, "But without faith it is impossible to please Him; for they that come to God must believe that He is, and He is the rewarder of them that diligently seek Him." Seeking God diligently begins in your heart. It begins with having confidence in God; having assurance in Him. With the same confidence you focus on where God says He is taking you. With that assurance you focus and aim for what God is leading you to, what He is showing you or speaking to you of. Faith sees what God has said and focuses on it. So, you seek God with confidence, willing to let go of anything in order to see His glory manifested, which is bigger than anything you can imagine. If you seek God whole heartedly you must know He will reward your faith.

Hebrews 10:35, says, "Cast not away therefore your confidence, which hath great recompense of reward." Goliath was not a problem to David, because beyond Goliath David inside was focusing on what God had said and promised. Goliath was to him, just one of the stepping stones to the mountain top. That is why after killing Goliath,

David started facing some trials. Those trials were to prepare him for elevation and dominion. God did not allow the faith of David to immediately move away the mountain of his trials. He allowed him to climb that mountain till he reached the mountain top where he was able to see clearly. To see clearly is to understand that without Christ we can do nothing. That without Him we are nothing. But through Him we can do all things.

Hebrews 11:1 says, "Faith is the substance of things hoped for, the evidence of things not seen." Substance and evidence are things you can see. The essential meaning of these words is that faith is active. When someone is walking by faith there is something you will see that shows you their assurance for what they are expecting. Even if you are alone, your own actions and words will show you if you are in faith or not. It will be clear. Where there is faith there is bold confessions and actions. David with boldness looked at Goliath and said, "This day will the Lord deliver thee into mine hand; and I will smite thee, and take thine head from thee; and I will give the carcases of the host of the philistines this day unto the fowls of the air"-1 Samuel 17:46. In 1 Samuel 17:48 it says, "And it came to pass, when the philistine arose, and came and drew nigh to meet David, that David hasted, and ran towards the army to meet the philistine." David in this battle spoke boldly and acted boldly because knew the results. Our faith is the evidence of what has already happened or been given in the spirit. That means a man of faith is more conscious of the spirit realm than he is of the physical realm.

Faith is depending on God in order to please Him. Faith is not labouring through your flesh/ works to please God. Our labour is in faith and faith is looking at Him not us. If we please God through our labour of the flesh then who gets the credit? But if we please Him by depending on Him then God gets the credit. God does not do this so that He can get the credit but because perfection is only found in Him. That is why if someone will depend on his own strength to lead his family he will surely fail and not know why. He will tell you I tried my best, but something went wrong. That is why even to have the ability to forgive others we need to depend on God. In John 6:29 Jesus said to his disciples, "This is the work of God, that you believe in Him whom He sent."

When we depend on God we celebrate Him more for His goodness and for what He does to us. But if we depend on our selves we want to celebrate what we do. That is why those who depend on their own goodness and strength get so offended if someone will criticise them as they do not want to be viewed by men as a people with faults. They want to be celebrated than they desire to see God celebrated. We must be careful of this because if we are not careful we will end up exchanging the glory of God for what is not glory (vain glory). Any time you want to depend on anything that is not

God, including ourselves, you exchange God's glory for what is not glory. God is looking for people who are so dependant on His goodness, His kindness and His mercy that they are waiting with expectation to celebrate His work in their lives. There is no one in the kingdom of God who is pleasing God without depending on Him.

In order for us to be pleasing we must be dependant and not try to be independent from Him. To be independent is to carry the burden that He said we must give to Him. There will be times that we are suppose to do things and we do not know how but He knows all the truth. We just need to depend on Him. It is like when you go to the doctor and he gives you a prescription. No matter what you thought, or what your friends and family said concerning your physical condition, you will rely on the doctor's prescription because of his training and experience. But Jesus did not have to be trained to know the truth. He is the eternal truth, the life and the way.

We must depend on God ever expecting with joy and thanksgiving to see and celebrate His goodness. Elijah was praying for rain and sent his servant to go and check. When the servant came back and said he sees a small cloud like the hand of man, Elijah ran and outran the king. He ran like that because he knew it was done. He honoured God on whom he was depending. That is equivalent to praise. It's like praying and then you feel a release in the spirit, and out of that you know it is done and you start praising. Great men of God on earth are those who depend more on God. Whenever we pray and praise before we see what we desire we do so in expectation. God does everything He does for His glory and to be celebrated, because He is the source of life and everything good. We have to purify our hearts and seek to give God all the glory and to see men celebrate Him. Offences and bitterness in our hearts can stop from glorifying Jesus. Offences and bitterness makes us to focus on ourselves in stead of focusing on God and distract us from celebrating God and giving Him glory. We must humble ourselves and let go of offences and bitterness.

The Healing of Blind Bartimaeus (Mark 10:46):

I want to use the story of Bartimaeus as an example of persistent faith. Bartimaeus was a blind man, who sat by the high way begging for alms. One day this man heard that Jesus was passing by, going out of Jericho. When he heard that Jesus was passing he began to cry out, "Jesus, son of David, have mercy on me." Many at that time began to shut him up. The bible says many, not one or few, told him to be quiet. Bartimaeus had a disability. He could not see. That means he couldn't see exactly where Jesus was standing so that he could just run to him.

The woman with the issue of blood had a serious problem but she could at least see Jesus. So she said to herself, if only I can just touch the hem of his garment I shall be made whole. But Bartimaeus couldn't see; so he couldn't even do that. He probably said to himself, "I can not see but I can use my voice to call. I can not be able to run to him, to reach to him or to touch him. I have this limitation, but I can call on Him. Though I can not reach Him, if He can hear me He will help me." I believe he said to himself, "I have no choice but to call on Him." The people that discouraged Bartimaeus from calling could see that he had a problem and they knew that Jesus had the solution. In stead of encouraging the man's faith or helping him to come to Jesus, they said to him, "Hold your peace." The bible says, Bartimaeus cried the more a great deal, Son of David, have mercy on me. He understood that God is a merciful God, and that is the secret code (the key) of David; the revelation of God's mercy, righteousness and justice. David ruled over Israel with this revelation.

And Jesus, in spite of all their attitudes towards Bartimaeus, stood still and commanded him to be called. And now people turned to him and said, cheer up; He is calling you. They even said "cheer up" because they knew that his problem was over. Bartimaeus was ready because he was so focused on Jesus. The moment they said he is calling you he threw off his garment, rose and came to Jesus. That is like putting off the slave mentality of the position you have been in. A slave does not think he has the right to say what he wants. He only accepts whatever comes. And so, Jesus did not just lay hands on him though He knew his problem. He asked him, first, "what do you want me to do for you?" Bartimaeus did not hesitate. He said, I want

108

to see again/ that I may receive my sight. And Jesus said to him, go your way; your faith has made you whole. Bartimaeus immediately received his sight and followed Jesus in the way. Many prior to that looked at Bartimaeus and saw a useless, blind man who was not worthy of the attention of such an important man like Jesus. To them he was not worthy of what he was asking for. But Jesus looked at Bartimaeus and saw the beauty of faith. So, Jesus did not focus on the attitudes of people but on the faith of Bartimaeus.

All this was happening before Jesus died on the cross, to pay the price for our redemption. Now Jesus has paid the price for our freedom. We have even more reason to believe. Bartimaeus said what he wanted knowing Jesus was able to do it for him. We confess today by faith, what has already been fulfilled. *So faith is saying with confidence what you want to see manifest, knowing every good thing you need from God has already been given. It is His pleasure to see His will manifested in your life.*

When you are seeking the Lord, it does not matter who does not believe in you or in your faith. Don't be discouraged or distracted by the resistance or attitudes of those who do not believe in your faith because God believes in your faith. This is very important because your faith is an expression of what you see for your future. You must not let anyone make you set the standard low for yourself. It is what you see that matters. That is why we are instructed to put on the belt of truth. The truth is not necessarily physical reality. The truth is what God has said and done in the realm of the Spirit.

Pilate said to Jesus, "Don't you know that I have power to crucify you or to release you?" Jesus told Him the truth. He said to him, "You would have no authority over me unless it was given you from above."

Before David faced Goliath, his own older brother, Eliab, spoke against him. He did not believe in him and he tried to put him down. He said, "Why did you come down here? And with whom have you left those few sheep in the wilderness? I know your pride and the insolence of your heart, for you have come down to see the battle."-1 Samuel 17:28. That was almost like trying to make him feel bad about himself; like he was in the wrong place. But as the scripture says, David did not waste time disputing with him. He just made his point that he had done nothing wrong and that there was a cause for his coming. And immediately he turned from him and continued talking with those he could speak faith/ express his faith to. David was a man focused on the Lord. Just like Bartimaeus he did not waste time paying attention on the resistance of those who did not believe in him or his faith. He focused on God and pressed on with faith. It is important in life not to waste time paying attention on people who do not have your best interest in heart nor believe in your faith. It does not matter how low they try to push you; Jesus will lift you up. Be bold and look beyond them, because the one you really need cares for you and for your best interest. Wicked people are, even more wicked to you, when they think you need them. Like Bartimaeus, focus on the constant love, mercies, compassion, grace and the righteousness of God.

Finally David faced Goliath. And without wavering he said to Goliath, "You come against me with a sword, and with a spear, and with a shield: but I come to you in the name of the Lord of hosts, the God of the armies of Israel, whom you have defiled. This day will the Lord deliver you into my hand; and I will smite you and take your head from you; and I will give the carcases of the host of the philistines this day unto the fowls of the air and to the wild beasts of the earth; that all the earth may know that there is a God in Israel."- 1 Samuel 17:45-46. David was saying all this to Goliath who was not only a giant but was wearing a strong armour and whose sword was like a weaver's beam. David himself on the other hand had not even a sword in his hand, but to him the battle was already won. And his reason for that was he was coming in the name of the Lord and he was not leaning on natural efforts and means. With faith someone is able to move without fear of anything, like a baby that is ever expecting good.

Jesus did not say, when the Son of man comes, will He find people who are like this or that. He said, "when the Son of man comes, shall He find faith on earth."-Luke18:8. Prophet Manasseh Jordan once said, "Faith is not what you are trying to get from God, but what you are willing to give away to Him." That means because God has already given us all things in Christ, in faith we always let go of something in order to gain Christ and to see the manifestation of what He has given already. Some have to let go of fear and doubt; some have to let go of their trust in people or in material things. When we do so we draw near to God and we find

ourselves in a place where we are able to operate
with God's power.

Fighting the Good Fight of Faith:

Everyone who receives Jesus Christ receives eternal
life. Sin and death do not have dominion over him.
However everyone who is born of God is constantly
in a fight and that fight is a fight of faith. Every child
of God has a personal responsibility to fight the
good fight of faith. Satan has no power and no
authority over the church but he uses his whiles to
fight the church. He uses them to try and fight the
faith of believers. He knows that if we receive and
believe what the word says we will have what the
word guarantees. We are destined to possess what
God has given us but we possess it by faith.

In 2 Timothy 4:7, Paul says, "I have fought the good
fight, I have finished my course, I have kept the
faith:" We all have a race before us to run; a course
before us to complete. In order to finish our course
we need to fight the good fight and we need to
keep the faith. Faith comes by hearing the word of
God; so to fight the good fight of faith we need the
word and we need to stick with the word. In
1Timothy 6:12, says, "Fight the good fight of faith,
lay hold on eternal life, whereunto thou art also
called, and hast professed a good profession before
many witnesses." What is eternal life? Eternal life is

the life God has given to the church, not to the world. The word of God helps us understand that what eternal life entails. The word reveals to us what God has established for us in the spirit.

In Psalm 119:89, says, "For ever, o Lord thy word is settled in heaven." The word of God is everything we need. The word of God is steadfast and it is faithful. It is settled; it can not be moved; it can not be changed. 2 Corinthians 1:20, says, "For all the promises of God in Him (Jesus) are yea, and in Him Amen, unto the glory of God by us." When every one and everything says otherwise the truth is what the word says.

Before Jesus came there was enough to disqualify everyone from attaining any of the promises of God. But through Jesus God has qualified us. 2 Corinthians 1:19, says, "For the Son of God, Jesus Christ, who was preached among you by us, even by me and Silvanus and Timotheus, was not yea and nay, but in Him was yea." Even when everything says no, the promises of God in Jesus are yes to us. Where everyone and everything says no to us Jesus says yes. He says yes, to bring to pass the promises of God in our lives; that means to bring to pass the will of God. To fight the good fight of faith is to agree with Jesus even if it does not make sense; even if people do not agree with you; even if nobody says yes and amen.

In 1Timothy 1:18, Paul says, "This charge I commit unto thee, son Timothy, according to the prophecies, which went before on thee, that thou by them mightest war a good warfare; holding faith, and a good conscience; which some having put away have made a shipwreck:" Paul here is charging Timothy to fight the good fight of faith according to the prophesies that went before him. That means by faith he must hold on to the prophecies spoken over him. Paul in this verse instructs Timothy that in order to achieve this he must hold faith and a good conscience. That means he must respect and believe the word and the prophecies and he must keep a good conscience. In order to believe the word one must refuse to meditate on the natural negative happenings and negative confessions of others. The result is you constantly see inside what God has said and promised and you confess it boldly.

 The second thing he said is hold a good conscience. The enemy of good conscience is guilt and condemnation. They rob someone of the opportunity to look at himself the way God looks at him. This usually causes a man to be constantly filled with sorrow. So it means you have authority and victory but you are weakened by guilt and condemnation which affects even your thoughts. You need to remove guilt and condemnation through the word and right confessions. But in order to keep a good conscience, firstly you must stay away from the company of those who are always judging you, accusing you and condemning you. They will not teach you the will of God for you. They will say things that will pull you down and away from the will of God, and suck your confidence in God and in His love for you. That can not be the will of God for you. If they by any chance make negative comments reject them instantly from your system. Do not retain them; they do no benefit you.

One of the blunders in the church is when brothers and sisters accuse and point fingers on other brothers and sisters. They make comments without knowing what their brother or sister is dealing with. They have expectations on their fellow brothers and sisters and when their expectations are not met they turn into accusers, which is satan's role and they want to judge like God. God alone is the judge and He has no assistant in that department. That position will forever be vacant. Those who accuse fellow believers weaken their brother and sister through the deception of guilt and condemnation. They pull down even those who are wounded. Job in Job19:28, says, "But ye should say, why persecute we him, seeing the root of the matter is found in me? Be ye afraid of the sword: for wrath bringeth the punishments of the sword, that ye may know there is a judgement."

In all that we do we must know that the judge of man is God. The attitude of the accusers can deceive the one who is accused into guilt and a bad conscience. That is when you have to fight to keep a good conscience. A good conscience is your priority in this case. If you have to lose their friendship it is ok. Separate yourself and if they hate you it is ok. If they gather against you do not be afraid. Let them do what they do but stay focused. Those who live to please people this will create a stronghold in them. Whoever keeps a good conscience in spite of everything is wise. You are not made by the approval or acceptance of people but by the word of God. Even if your accusers are very respected by people and are in the house of God, God will still be with you and promote you in spite of their accusations.

1 Peter 3:16 says, "Having a good conscience; that whereas they speak evil of you, as of evil doers, they may be ashamed that falsely accuse your good conversation in Christ." Our good conversation is our walk in love. This is to understand the perfect will of God. We do not owe people that we should please them at the expense of our conscience and we do not owe the flesh to be affected by its works. And satan because he is the accuser he will try to push you to focus on works of the flesh through condemnation and guilt. But thank God we know the truth and we are strengthened. Romans 8:1,

says, "There is therefore now no more condemnation to them which are in Christ, who walk not after the flesh, but after the spirit." They do not mind the things of the flesh but of the spirit. Romans 8:12, says, "Therefore, brethren, we are not debtors, not to the flesh, to live after the flesh."

To fight the good fight of faith is to focus on what the word of God says and say it with boldness. It is to say the same thing in agreement with God in spite of what you see with your physical eyes. It is to be steadfast, unmovable and persistent in your confessions of faith. Where satan wants you to say no you say yes. Where satan wants you to be discouraged you declare the word and what God is saying in the spirit, with boldness. Refuse to fear. Somebody said fear is faith in reverse. You fear that something bad will happen because you believe more in the power of satan than the power of God in that situation. God has no limits except the ones we give Him.

The word of God is all powerful and in order to win the fight of faith we need to be able to control our thoughts and align them with the word of God. There are people who have no control over their thoughts. Everything every where affects their thinking. They pray with faith at home and then they come into a taxi or bus or train, and hear something that affects their thinking and their faith. The danger with that is that their lives get impacted negatively because our lives go in the direction of our thoughts because of the law of faith. Those who have no control over their own thoughts are easy prey to the devil. That is why we need to meditate on the word of God always. We must sow the word of God in yourself. Psalm 126:5, says, "They that sow in tears shall reap in joy. He that goeth forth and weepeth, bearing precious seed, shall doubtless come again with rejoicing, bringing his sheaves with him."

One very important thing to mention as we talk about the good fight of faith is our dreams. Job said in Job 7:13, "When I say, my bed shall comfort me, my couch shall ease my complaint; then thou scarest me with dreams, and terrifiest me through visions:" This means Job was not having good dreams during that time of his trails. May be his dreams were so discouraging. If you are going through some challenges in the physical and when you go to sleep, you dream being defeated, being disqualified, getting no where, or being overtaken by everybody, that is not a good dream to have. Dreams are like images given to you for free to direct your imagination. And your imaginative power is your creative ability. Therefore if you spend time thinking about the bad things you dreamt of you will start imagining those things happening to you. Some people when they have bad dreams they start fearing that those things they see in dreams will happen to them, and that is negative faith.

We need to understand that the word of God has authority. It has power even over the evil that we see in the spirit. If you dream being defeated you must wake up and say I am more than a conqueror. If you dream being disqualified, you must wake up and say, there is no more condemnation to me because I am in Christ. To Jairus, whose daughter had died Jesus said Fear not: believe only, and she shall be made whole. And Isaiah 54:17, says, "No weapon that is formed against thee shall be able to prosper, and every tongue that shall rise against thee in judgement thou shalt condemn. That mans nothing done against you has any power to prosper but you have power to condemn every verdict of the enemy. If the verdict of the enemy is condemned then it does not stand. We have authority in the name of Jesus. And remember satan's aim is to try and get many to believe and focus on what is not true. That is why the word is so necessary.

Psalm 4:4, says, "Stand in awe, and sin not: Commune with your heart upon your bed and be still." Stand in awe means stand in honour. That means you constantly remember the works of God and honour them. That means remember the works of God and don't be in unbelief or in doubt. He says commune with your heart and be still. It means you talk to your heart of the word and the works of God and rest in Him because of faith. Psalm 33:4 says, "For the word of the Lord is right: and all His works are done in truth." This is important because when we remember the works of God we are encouraged to believe more. And when we talk to our hearts concerning His word and His works we are able to rejoice in peace and in faith. There is nothing any one can do to change the word of God and to reverse the works of God.

1Corinthians 15:57, says, "But thanks be to God, which giveth us the victory through our Lord Jesus Christ." By this it is clear that our victory is through the lord Jesus.

Prevailing in Warfare:

Satan throws the worst attacks when he sees you are about to get your best victory. But we win through the power of the word of God. The mature saint speaks the word with faith and is undeterred. Discouragement is the song of the enemy against those who are facing the right direction and are determined. But we fight the good fight of faith, knowing that God is on the side of the just and He favours them. We have overcome the enemy because we know the truth. We reign through the Word of God.

As long as we put on the whole armour of God satan has no chance. Ephesians 6:12 says, "For we wrestle not against flesh and blood, but against principalities, against powers, against the rulers of the darkness of this world, against spiritual wickedness in high places. Wherefore take unto you the whole armour of God, that ye may be able to withstand in the evil day, and having done all to stand."

We put on the breast plate of righteousness: that means our conscience is clear of guilt through the consciousness of the righteousness of God.

We put on the belt of truth: We strengthen ourselves through the knowledge of the truth (the word) and by the revelations He gives us. That is why it is important to meditate on the word of God.

We put on our feet the preparation of the gospel: that means we are ready to answer everyone that asks us the reason for our hope in Christ.

We put on the shield of faith: that means we refuse to believe, think or speak anything contrary to the word of God. We believe the Word.

We put on the helmet of salvation: we stay under the blood and lean on the power of the name of Jesus that saved us through faith. WE lean on the covenant of God through Jesus.

We use the sword of the spirit: that is declaring and confessing the word, creating change by the authority given to us by Jesus.

It does not matter if your enemy is poverty, lack, sickness or confusion. You have been given power over it in the name of Jesus. You should never be afraid of any of these things. You are too high for your enemy, because of who you are by grace. We do not win in life because we fight a lot but because of faith; because we fight the good fight of faith. Everything that is ours has been redeemed for us by Jesus.

Four very important questions to ask ourselves are; who is the Christian? Where is he? What does he have? And what does he have to do?

Who is the Christian? - He is the righteousness of God. He is an offspring of God. He is one whose name is written in the book of the Lamb of God; one who has Christ living in him; one who lives by faith. One who is born of the Word of God. He is a king and a priest unto God. Revelations 5:9 says, "And they sung a new song, saying, thou art worthy to take the book, and open the seals thereof: for thou wast slain, and redeemed us to God by thy blood out of every kindred, and tongue, and people, and nation. And hast made us unto our God kings and priests: and we shall reign on earth"

Where is he? - He is sited in the heavenly places with Christ. He is alive in the more powerful realm; the realm of the spirit. He is hidden with Christ in

God. He is in the company of angels. He is in Christ. He is in mount Zion.

What does he have? - He has the life of God in abundance/ eternal life. He has all things pertaining to life and godliness. He has inherited the world. He has authority to reign in life and over all the power of satan. He has the anointing of the spirit of God. He has the wisdom of God. He has faith. He has victory. The Christian has power to change things.

What does the Christian have to do? – To renew his mind and align with word of God. He needs to have the mind of Christ. He has to see things differently from the world. He has to walk as Jesus walked, with authority and submission. He has to fulfil his purpose as an ambassador of the kingdom of God, as Jesus fulfilled His. He has to live his life for Christ, not for himself. He must cast out satan wherever he finds him. He has to follow Jesus.

I can not close this topic without talking about the future of a Christian, as intended by God. The eternal future of a Christian, as intended by God, is far beyond what the human spirit can fully conceive. It is too glorious for the eyes of the human mind to see. It is too beautiful for the heart of man to contain. In 1 Corinthians 6:2, Paul says, "Do ye not know that the saints shall judge the world? And if the world shall be judged by you, are ye unworthy to judge the smallest matters?" In Daniel 7:27, Daniel is told in a vision, "And the kingdom and dominion, and the greatness of the kingdom under the whole heaven shall be given to the people of the saints of the most High, whose kingdom is an everlasting kingdom, and all dominions shall serve and obey Him."

Turn on the Power:

It is like having a cell phone which has a battery that is fully charged but the cell phone is off. Meaning thou the battery is fully charged the phone is not functional because it is off. There is a button on the phone that when you press the power in the battery is activated and it causes the phone to light up and function. When the battery is flat the phone that is fully equipped to function will not function. Therefore if such a phone has a battery that is fully charged all that remains is to press the button to turn on the power. As children of God in order to activate or turn on the power inside we need to arise with faith. We activate it by faith. This power is turned on through faith and expectancy. What we expect is what we hope to see. What you expect is what you see in your heart and faith is the button you press to turn on the power. That means we connect our faith to something we see inside.

Facing Giants:

Some times in life we deal with situations that are orchestrated by demons that are standing against us as giants. It is obvious that they will stand with everything they can against those who they consider giants in the kingdom of God. No matter what spirit stands as a giant against us it is already defeated and is under our feet. Every one who faces some very stubborn giants has a very important role in society. One of the aims of these giants is to make such a person give up and to destroy him if possible. Those who overcome are those who see and confess victory always. It is through knowledge that we are able to destroy their snares and power.

There are six things that are important when dealing with giants. They are;

1.   **Faith**: Faith is the power button that activates and releases the power in your life. Faith itself comes through the light of the knowledge of the word of God.

2.   **The love of God**: The love of God helps us to be stable, confident and at peace in spite of what is front of us. What can not stand against God can not stand against us if God is on our side. That is why

the word says, "What shall we then say to these things? If God is for us, who can be against us?"- Romans 8:31.

3.   **Purpose**: Purpose is what you live for. It is what you see in your heart day and night. It is what helps you to be true to yourself and to be authentic.

4.   **Power within you**: God gave us power by His Spirit because He knew we would face demonic forces and powers. He gave us power over them.

5.   **Praise and worship**: Through praise and worship we magnify the Lord, not situations or demons.

6.   **Courage and determination**: These two qualities help you to never look back but to confront challenges without hesitation or intimidation.

David is a good example of a man who faced and overcame a giant without struggle. David refused to fear goliath and encouraged others not to be afraid of him. He had a different perception of goliath. Everyone was looking at goliath as a giant who was heavily armed and well trained to fight. Meaning according to them it was impossible to overcome him. And of truth it was naturally difficult to defeat goliath. David on the other hand was not bothered by the size of goliath, or by his armour or how well trained he was. He was not looking at goliath only physically but spiritually. Spiritually David was a giant over goliath. This is why David repeatedly tried to make this point; that goliath was an uncircumcised philistine. David testified with his own mouth that it was not the first time he faced physical giants. He had killed the lion and the bear before. Both these animals are strong and powerful physically and they are naturally designed to fight. If he killed them it is obvious that the hand of the Lord was there to deliver him. He had already experienced miracles where God destroyed giants before him.

David also refused to put on a physical armour, even thou goliath was wearing one. But the truth is David was putting on spiritual armour. The first thing was he overcame discouragement from his brother and from Saul, through faith. The accusation of his brother could do him no harm because he was putting on the breast plate of righteousness. When goliath tried to curse him it could not work because he was wearing a helmet of salvation. When goliath tried to prophesy his own victory against David but David was strengthened by the belt of truth. And because of the preparation of the gospel on his feet he was testifying the good news to the army of Israel even before he killed goliath. The next thing David did was to prophesy and confess his own victory against goliath. And the last thing he did was to move towards goliath with courage and determination and defeated him and goliath could not touch David once.

One of the issues the church has is the issue of position. Revelations 1:6, says, "He has made us kings and priests". We are God's servants with authority. We are approach God with confidence. Even in brokenness we are not afraid, for we have received the Spirit of power, of love and of sound mind. We do not look at any situation from the position of fear and defeat but from a position of authority. We put on the whole armour and stand in the position of authority.

The children of Israel looked at Goliath from a position of fear and defeat. They were weakened and paralysed by fear, because they were in the wrong position. David on the other hand came against him from a different position and he came wearing the armour of God. That is why he said, "You come against me with sword and spear and javelin, but I come against you in the name of the LORD Almighty, the God of the armies of Israel, whom you have defied."- 1 Samuel 17:45.

David said, "who *is* this uncircumcised Philistine, that he should defy the armies of the living God?"- 1Samuel 17:6. That is the helmet of salvation, and it speaks of covenant. Goliath's covenant was nothing to match the covenant that God had with Israel; that is what David was saying. In verse 45, he said,

"Then all this assembly shall know that the Lord does not save with sword and spear; for the battle *is* the Lord's, and He will give you into our hands." This is an indication that his feet were shod/ equipped with the preparation of the gospel. The gospel is the good news. The good news David was preaching was that God does not need physical weapons to save. He was declaring that God has already given authority over their enemies.

In verse 32, we hear the audacity of David's faith. He said, "Let no man's heart fail because of him; your servant will go and fight with this Philistine." He was wearing a shield of faith, protecting him from the lies of Satan and he had no fear of the enemy in front of him. In verse 45, he said, "You come against me with sword and spear and javelin, but I come against you in the name of the LORD Almighty, the God of the armies of Israel, whom you have defied." This is an indication that he had a revelation about the truth. He was not focusing on what is seen with physical eyes but on the truth revealed by God. He was strengthened by the belt of truth. In verse 46, David says to the Philistine, "This day the Lord will deliver you into my hand, and I will strike you and take your head from you. And this day I will give the carcasses of the camp of the Philistines to the birds of the air and the wild beasts of the earth, that all the earth may know that there is a God in Israel." He was using the sword of the Spirit which is the word. This is the sword that destroyed Goliath.

Before David faced Goliath his own brother stood against him; "Now Eliab his oldest brother heard when he spoke to the men; and Eliab's anger was aroused against David, and he said, "Why did you come down here? And with whom have you left those few sheep in the wilderness? I know your pride and the insolence of your heart, for you have come down to see the battle." And David said, "What have I done now? Is *there* not a cause?" Then he turned from him toward another and said the same thing; and these people answered him as the first ones *did.*" David was not discouraged by his brother's behaviour and words because he was wearing the breast plate of righteousness. He did not accumulate guilt from the judgement of his brother.

For those of us who are born again the revelation in the knowledge of the love and authority of Jesus, whose body we are, helps us to stand strong and courageous. He gave Himself as a lamb for us with great love. John 15:15, says, "Greater love has no one than this: to lay down one's life for one's friends." If He has loved us enough to lay down His life for us He surely loves us enough to deliver us from anything. As a king He reigns over everything in heaven and on earth and under the earth. Ephesians 1:18-23, says, "the eyes of your understanding being enlightened; that you may know what is the hope of His calling, what are the riches of the glory of His inheritance in the saints, and what *is* the exceeding greatness of His power toward us who believe, according to the working of His mighty power which He worked in Christ when He raised Him from the dead and seated *Him* at His right hand in the heavenly *places,* far above all principality and power and might and dominion, and every name that is named, not only in this age but also in that which is to come." 1 Corinthians 15:27, says, "For He has put all things under His feet." But when He says "all things are put under *Him,*" *it is* evident that He who put all things under Him is excepted."

The Power of Faith and Love:

Galatians 5:6 says, "For in Jesus Christ neither circumcision availeth any thing, nor uncircumcision; but faith which worketh by love." That means the end results of true faith in Christ is walking in love. Faith empowers you to love others. This ultimately empowers you to follow what I call the principle of life. The principle of life is this; "As long as the earth remains seed time and harvest will never cease." Jesus put it this way; in Matthew 7:11 He says, "If ye then being evil know how to give good gifts to your children, how much more shall your Father which is in heaven give good things to them that ask Him? Therefore all things whatsoever ye would that men should do to you, do ye even so to them: for this is the law and prophets." He starts by showing us that whatever we desire of the Father there is guarantee that He will give because He is a good God. But then He adds and gives us this principle; whatever we want others to do to us that we must do to them. This scripture shows us that we are empowered to treat others well because of our faith in a God who is good.

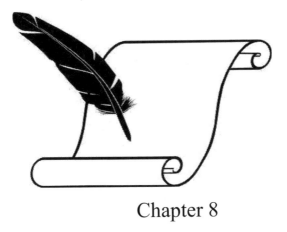

Chapter 8

FELLOWSHIP

To the Corinthians Paul said, "God is faithful, who has called you into fellowship with his Son, Jesus Christ our Lord." - 1 Corinthians 1:9. God has called us to have a relationship with Him, which is cultivated through the fellowship we have with Him and with other believers.

In Colossians 3:16, he says, "Let the word of Christ dwell in you richly in all wisdom, teaching and admonishing one another in psalms and hymns and spiritual songs, singing with grace in your hearts to the Lord." This simply refers to building one another's faith through fellowship with brothers and sisters.

Prayer:

Through prayer we communicate and fellowship with God by faith. It is more of fellowship with God than it is about just asking God for something. Through prayer we are also able stir up the gifts of the spirit and to activate the power we have received by His Spirit.

And by the power of the Holy Spirit we are able to effect change in the natural declarations (faith-filled words). Kings 13:3-4, says, "Then he gave a sign the same day, saying, "This is the sign which the LORD has spoken, 'Behold, the altar shall be split apart and the ashes which are on it shall be poured out.' "Now when the king heard the saying of the man of God, which he cried against the altar in Bethel, Jeroboam stretched out his hand from the altar, saying, "Seize him." But his hand which he stretched out against him dried up, so that he could not draw it back to himself. The altar also was split apart and the ashes were poured out from the altar, according to the sign which the man of God had given by the word of the LORD...." This is the power of words spoken in faith.

There are four types of prayers one can engage in, which involve communication and fellowship with God;

1.   **The first is praise**: This is part of fellowship in which you give thanks to God for He is for ever merciful, gracious, good, patient, faithful, righteous and full of truth. We must always approach the Lord with thanksgiving. Psalm 100:4, says, "Enter in to His gates with thanksgiving, and into His courts

with praise: be thankful unto Him, and bless His name."

2. **The second is worship**: Worship is the practice adoring the beauty of God's glory. Lifting up His name for He is seated upon the throne and He reigns over all His creation in heaven, in earth and under the earth. We worship Him because He is holy. The closer we get to the Lord is more we know Him and worship Him.

3. **The third is intercession for others**: This is when we stand in the gap for other people and nations, before God. We call on the Lord on their behalf. God is always looking for a man to stand in the gap for others. Sometimes God Himself leads us on who to pray for and what to pray for.

4. **The fourth is of making petitions to God for whatever we desire of Him**: James 5:13, says, "Is any among you afflicted? Let him pray. Is any merry? Let him sing psalms." Philippians 4:6, says, "Be anxious for nothing, but in everything by prayer and supplication, with thanksgiving, let your requests be made known to God;" Speaking of Jesus Hebrews 5:7, says, "who, in the days of His flesh, when He had offered up prayers and supplications, with vehement cries and tears to Him who was able to save Him from death, and was heard because of His godly fear."

Apart from all these types of prayers those who are baptized with the Holy Spirit (in tongues) are able to pray also in the spirit, which is praying not according to understanding.

Jude 1:20 says, "But you, dear friends, by building yourselves up in your most holy faith and praying in the Holy Spirit," 1 Corinthians 14:15, says, "For if I pray in a tongue, my spirit prays, but my mind is unfruitful. What then shall I do? I will pray with my spirit, but I will also pray with my mind. I will sing with my spirit, but I will also sing with my mind."

In Mark 11:23-25, Jesus points out three very important things we must observe when we pray. He says in these verses, "For verily I say unto you, that whosoever shall say unto this mountain, be thou removed, and be thou cast into the sea; and shall not doubt in his heart, but shall believe that those things which he saith shall come to pass; he shall have whatsoever he saith. Therefore I say unto you, what things soever ye desire, when ye pray, believe that ye receive them and ye shall have them. And when ye stand praying, forgive, if ye have ought against any: that your Father also which is in heaven may forgive you your trespasses."

The first thing we must observe is that because there is power in the name of Jesus, whatever we decree or command in the spirit, we must believe that it shall come to pass and we must not doubt. If we are asking something from the Lord we must believe that we are receiving while praying, because the Lord hears and He knows even what is in our hearts. Because he is faithful, He responds to our faith immediately when we pray. If we believe we have received we will see what we prayed for. The second thing is that when we decree things or make petitions to the Lord we must first know exactly what we desire, because what we desire is what shall be granted or come to pass. The third thing is that we must not pray with issues, grudges and unforgiveness in our hearts. If there is anyone who has done us wrong we ought to give the issue to the Lord and forgive them. God is love and He does not change. His anointing flows in love. All our prayers must be done in love.

When you pray, or praise or worship, God does not look at your mouth, or your tongue or how your lips are moving. He looks at your heart. When Jesus was praying at the garden of Gethsemane Peter heard Him repeat the same thing over and over. He wondered because he kept hearing Jesus saying, "If you are willing let this cup pass from me." Jesus repeated those words not because he was trying to convince God with repetition but because he was very sorrowful. He had a burden in His heart. He was pouring out His heart to the father. As a result an angel appeared to Him from heaven to strengthen Him. That means when we pray with a burden inside, we must pray until we feel the release in the spirit. When you pray with a burden in your heart, it is like your heart is trying to reach out to the heart of God, and that really moves God. And that's why this kind of prayer gets immediate results.

Praise:

David, in psalm 47:7 said, "sing ye praises with understanding." What this implies is that we are able to praise the Lord as we should when we have understanding. It means praising God with revelation in the knowledge of Him which makes it inevitable to praise Him. In Psalm 92:6, the psalmist says, "A brutish man knoweth not; neither doth a fool understand this."

Once you have revelation of the Lord; His might, His mercy, His goodness, His righteousness, His truth and His loving kindness, praise will flow naturally. When we praise God we show forth His loving kindness and faithfulness according to psalm 92:1-2. Psalm 145:6, says, "And men shall speak of the might of thy terrible acts: and I will declare thy greatness. They shall abundantly utter the memory of thy great goodness, and shall sing of thy righteousness. The Lord is gracious, and full of compassion: slow to anger, and of great mercy." When we sing to the Lord and bless His name we show forth His salvation. We declare His glorious work on earth. We praise Him with joy, not only for an answered prayer but because we know His constant loving kindness. We bring a sacrifice of praise and an offering because we are so grateful to Him. It is only because of Him, that we can have what we can never ever deserve. We rejoice before Him in the knowledge of His righteousness.-(Psalm 96). All this we receive and understand by faith.

We praise Him even more because we understand that it is not because we are good or perfect but because He is good. We praise Him with assurance that we will always experience His power and His goodness and that He will always be with us. We understand that He reigns over all the earth, in righteousness and in the abundance of His goodness He is merciful towards all men. In Him is all truth.

The mercies and justice of God culminates in two ways on earth; one is when He justifies those who believe in Jesus, apart from their own works. Therefore, Hebrews 13:15, says, "By Him (Jesus) therefore let us offer the sacrifice of praise to God continually, that is, the fruit of our lips giving thanks to His name." Number two, is when He lifts up one who is broken, forsaken and forgotten, and sets him high. Psalm 113:3, says, "From the rising of the sun unto the going down of the same the Lord's name is to be prised. The Lord is high above all nations, and His glory above the heavens. Who is like unto the Lord our God, who dwells on high, who humbles Himself to behold the things that are in heaven, and in earth! He rises up the poor out of the dust, and lifts the needy out of the dunghill; That He may set the princes, even with the princes of his people. He makes the barren woman to keep house, and to be a joyful mother of children, praise ye the Lord.

We praise God for His holiness. Because He is holy He is too perfect to make any error and He is good to us even when we are imperfect. Psalm 97:12, says, "Rejoice in the Lord, ye righteous and give thanks at the remembrance of His holiness." We need to constantly be conscious of His holiness/perfection. Psalm 93:5, says, "Thy testimonies are very sure: holiness becometh thine house, o Lord forever." That means He dwells in holiness/perfection forever. It is impossible to ever find a spot of error in Him. The totality of the essence of His being and His dwelling is holiness/perfection.

We are suppose to praise the Lord with our voices, with a shout, with a clap, with a dance and with any instrument we possibly can. We praise Him because we understand that His works and His thoughts towards us are constantly, in their depth, good and perfect. (Psalm 92:5)

We praise Him knowing He is on our side, in His strength, nomatter what we are dealing with, knowing that through Him we win always. (Psalm 95:4). With this knowledge we have hope for the future. We also praise Him because he has given us authority and nothing shall by any means hurt us. Psalm 149:6, says, "Let the high praises of God be in their mouth, and a two-edged sword in their hand: To execute vengeance upon the heathen, and punishments upon the people; to bind their kings with chains, and their nobles with fetters of iron; To execute upon them the judgement written: this honour have all His saints. Praise ye the Lord.

According to Psalm 95:1-3, We are suppose to praise the Lord with joy. We are suppose to make a joyful noise to Him. We praise Him with joy in hope and in faith. Praising Him with joy and in hope says it all. Praising Him with joy means you understand it is not about where you are but about God. It means you have gone past the level of building confidence in the knowledge of the will and the goodness of God, to thanking Him for the same. Hebrews 3:6, says, "But Christ as a Son over His own house; whose house are we, if we hold fast the confidence and the rejoicing of the hope firm unto the end." Some body once said if you can praise God in the desert you can worship Him in the rain. We all know that God is good, but what makes Him good towards us is not that we are perfect, but His goodness, holiness, mercy and righteousness which we lift up when we praise Him. We rejoice because of this revelation; it is not an act when we rejoice. We understand that all power is in His hands and all knowledge is in Him. He knows the hearts of men. Yet He is good.

Psalm 95:7, says, "For He is our God; and we are the people of His pasture, and the sheep of His hand. Today if ye will hear His voice, harden not your heart, as in the provocation, and as in the day of temptation in the wilderness; when your fathers tempted me (They complained against God for needs), proved me (His power was manifested) and saw my work (His works were manifested). Forty years long was I grieved with this generation, and said, it is a people that do err in their heart, and they have not known my ways." That means the attitude of their heart was not right because they didn't know His thoughts, His attitude, the colour of His heart. They saw His works but never got to know His motives, His intensions and His heart. Through his encounter with Jesus, Paul had a revelation of the power and the goodness of God. When we know the thoughts of God towards us we praise in stead of complaining or being afraid.

Psalm 97:1, says, "The Lord reigneth: let the earth rejoice: let the multitudes of the isles be glad thereof." The earth must rejoice in the knowledge that the Lord reigns, because He reigns in righteousness.

Psalm 98:1, starts by saying, "Sing a new song to the Lord". All that the Lord does from season to season is because of His goodness and the excellence of His thoughts towards us. It is through His right hand and His Holy Arm that we get victory; because He is on our side. He keeps His mercy and truth towards us, because He is good and faithful. Therefore, we sing songs from season to season. We have a new song to sing to the Lord in every season because He is always doing something new. As His mercies are new every morning so are His acts and works in every season. We make a joyful noise before Him with this understanding. David in Psalm 34:1, says, "I will bless the Lord at all times. His praise shall continually be on my mouth." That means we have a lot to thank God for every time, because He is always doing great things.

We praise God because He is Holy (Perfect in totality), righteous in judgement, He is merciful (forgiving sin), and He is faithful (answering those that call upon Him night and day). We praise Him because we know that everything exist because He created it, in His might. He is exalted above all that exists and judges with justice, righteousness and mercy. The more we praise Him and declare His goodness and His greatness, and lift up His righteousness, is the more His glory manifests.

We praise God because we know who He is and His lovingkindness; We praise in spite of what we have or do not have. Nomatter how high God set us, we must continually offer the sacrifice of praise to Him and rejoice in His presence. In Psalm 108:1, David says, "O God, my heart is fixed; I will sing and give praise, even with my glory."

I will close this topic with Psalm 100;
"Make a joyful noise unto the Lord, all ye lands. Serve the Lord with gladness: it is He that hath made us, and not we ourselves; we are His people and sheep of His pasture. Enter into His gates with thanksgiving, and into His courts with praise: be thankful unto Him, and bless His name. For the Lord is good; His mercy is everlasting; and His truth endureth to all generations."

We must give thanks to God, King of all the Earth for:

- His presence and for His present help.
- His strength and power in us
- His faithfulness, patience, goodness, compassion, grace, mercy and truth.
- His steadfast love and covenant.
- The gift of righteousness
- His peace and His joy in us.
- His blessing and anointing upon us.

- Choosing us and causing us to draw near to Him.
- The gift of wisdom
- His victory given by His grace.
- Protecting and defending us.
- The ministry of angels
- Answering our prayers.
- Causing us to prosper and for promoting us by His favour.

Worship:

In John 4:21 Jesus said to the samaritan woman, "Woman, believe me, the hour cometh, when ye shall neither in this mountain, nor yet in Jerusalem, worship the Father. Ye worship ye know not what: we know what we worship: for salvation is of the Jews. But the hour cometh, and now is, when the true worshipers shall worship the Father in Spirit and in truth: for the Father seeketh such to worship Him." That simply means they will worship by the Spirit who leads us into all truth. Paul in 2 Timothy 1:7 says, "We have not received the Spirit of bondage to fear again, but the Spirit by which we cry abba father." By the spirit of the Lord we come before the throne of grace, and we worship Him in the beauty of His holiness. To Worship the Lord is to adore the beauty of His glory. The Psalmist in psalm 96:6, says, "Beauty and strength are in His

145

sanctuary." In His sanctuary there is beauty and strength beyond description. The Lord Himself is full of glory and strength.

When we worship the Lord we forget our own selves and surrender to Him because He alone is God in all the heavens and the earth. He sits upon the throne and reigns over all His creation. In Revelation 4:3, John says, "And immediately I was in the spirit: and, behold, a throne was set in heaven, and one sat on the throne."

In His presence we lift up His name, and give Him glory and honour. We sanctify His name in hearts. We forget ourselves and cast down everything about us before Him. Revelations 4:9, says, "And when those beasts give glory and honour and thanks to Him that sat on the throne, who liveth for ever and ever. The four and twenty elders fall down before Him that sat upon the throne, and worship Him that liveth for ever and ever, and cast their crowns before the throne, saying, thou art worthy, o Lord, to receive glory and honour and power: for thou hast created all things, and for thy pleasure they are and were created."

God is worthy to be worshiped by all His creation for ever and ever. Revelations 5:13, says, "And every creature which is in heaven, and on the earth, and under the earth, and such as are in the sea, and all that are in them, heard I saying, blessing, and honour, and glory and power, be unto Him that sitteth upon the throne, and unto the lamb for ever and ever." All the other gods are the works of man. The Lord is the Most High God. When He moves no one can resist Him. He has no equal. He has no competitor. His rivals are nothing before Him.

Chapter 9

THE CALL OF GOD

God is looking for people who will speak His truth, demonstrate His power, spread the light of His love and wisdom, and represent Him without compromise. He is looking for people He can use to manifest His glory.

The call of God is central to everyone's destiny on earth. Everyone who was used by God to do the work of the kingdom had a defining moment in which he had to say yes to the call of God. What the Lord calls us for ultimately become the vision for our life. That is why for everyone on earth to sincerely answer the call of God he/she must first clearly see, with conviction, what he/she is called to do; you sense a strong desire to play a certain role in life thou at first your intended approach to play that role may not be what God planned exactly. Mandela said when he was young and heard of all that was happening because of the tyranny over the black people in South Africa he hoped then that life would offer him an opportunity to serve his people. No wonder he made so much impact. His vision was clear to him.

Habakkuk 2:2 says, "And the Lord answered me and said, write the vision, and make it plain upon tables, that he may run with it that readeth." The visions for our lives from God are received by faith and the call of God is also answered by faith.

When you answer the call of God you give up some comfort in your life to gain what is glorious. In answering the call of God Abraham had to leave His father's house without knowing where he was going, having nothing to hold on to but the promises of God. Elisha gave up the comfort of his home and the work he was doing, to follow Elijah, without even knowing where Elijah was going next. Moses by faith gave up the comfort of being the son of Pharaoh's daughter. And the list goes on.

There are two men I know in the bible who were called differently. They were forcibly taken out of comfort and set on the path to fulfil their destiny. These two men are Joseph and Paul. Joseph saw visions and told his family and that lead to him being sold mischievously to be a slave. And in Egypt where he was a slave, God finally elevated him to fulfil his destiny.

Paul also while he was on his way to Damascus with a mission against the church, God interrupted his plans. He saw a bright light that was brighter than the sun, and because of that, he lost his sight. He was helped to come to a certain place in the street called straight and there he was three days in the presence of the Lord still blind. He temporarily lost the comfort of seeing with his physical eyes while God was speaking to him and showing him visions in the spirit.

There is also one man who had a very special call. This man is Abraham. In order to answer the call of God He had to submit directly to God when he left his father's house and there was no man he left submitted to or to submit to. He later met a man called Melchizedek who blessed him and he honoured the man with a tenth of all he had.- Genesis 14:18-20. This Melchizedek was a man without beginning and without ending. He was just as Jesus Himself. Abraham was also visited by two angels who were on the journey to Sodom and Gomorrah. These angels prophesied the birth of his son Isaac, who was the son of the promise.-Genesis 18:1-14, Hebrews 7:1-4.

Other men before Abraham, like Noah, also had a similar experience with God in their calling. But straight from Abraham's generation every man whose call was ever recorded in the bible had to be submitted to another man before he could himself be used by God or enter into the fulfilment of his assignment and destiny. Even Moses, had to serve Jethro his father in law, priest of Median, before he could be released to go and lead Israel out of captivity. I believe what was very special about the call of Abraham was that he was called to be the father of faith. He marked the generation of the children of faith. By faith we who believe are made heirs of the world with Abraham. So that where there is an inheritance, authority and protocol must be observed. Sons have an inheritance but bastards can not claim an inheritance. So then by faith we inherit what we have not laboured for because of covenant.

We also learn something in the book of Matthew. In order to give us the genealogy of Jesus, Matthew starts with Abraham and give us the descendants of Abraham until Jesus. This is in the first chapter of Matthew, from the first verse. We see that between Abraham and David there are fourteen generations. Between David and the carrying away to Babylon there are fourteen generations. And between the carrying away to Babylon and Jesus there are fourteen generations. These periods are separated by 14 generations and each mark something important. Abraham was called to be a father of many nations. So God didn't just say he would make his nation great but that He would make him the father of many nations. The meaning of that is that God will make him the father of the children of faith from every nation. So Abraham marks the opening of the door of faith which was fulfilled through Jesus.

David on the other hand was called and anointed to be king over Israel. God declared his throne an everlasting throne. David marked the release of a kingly anointing given to those who are in Christ today. Isaiah 55:3 says, "Incline your ear and come unto me: hear and your soul shall live; and I will make an everlasting covenant with you, even the sure mercies of David. Behold, I have given him for a witness to the people, a leader and commander to the people. Behold, thou shalt call a nation that knowest not thee shall run unto thee because of the Lord thy God, and for the Holy one of Israel; for He hath glorified thee."

The carrying away to Babylon marks the work of the spirit of mammon. But the significance here is that because of the kingly anointing the spirit of mammon is defeated. Every king has authority over the land and the resources thereof. All they have to do is decree what must be. Therefore kings can not be poor as long as there are resources in the land. After the birth of Jesus the first miracle that happened in His life was a miracle of financial prosperity. The wise men, who His parents did not know or invite had an encounter with angels who told them about of the King Jesus. They were lead to where he was by a star. When they arrived they worshipped Him and gave to His parents, gold, frankincense and myrrh. These were to honour the king Jesus. As a king He was attracting wealth already on the first day of His life on earth. His parents because of His birth were wealthy on His day of birth. The last one is Jesus. Jesus marks the perfect priesthood anointing. Hebrews 7:21, says, "For those priests were made without an oath; but this with an oath by Him that said unto Him, The Lord swear and will not repent, Thou art a priest for ever after the order of Melchizedek." Jesus is the king of kings, Lord of lords and the high priest according to the order of Melchizedek.

By faith Jesus was conceived. He was born a king, and during the time of His ministry He was referred to by many as the son of David. Because of the kingly anointing wealth was brought to Him by wise men, when He was still a small baby. And God in His wisdom made Him a high priest according to the order of Melchizedek.

For everyone on earth, the first step to answering the call of God is submission and humility. Elisha submitted to Elijah, Esther submitted to Modecai, Joshua submitted to Moses, Moses submitted to Jethro, Timothy submitted to Paul. And the list goes on. Even Jesus submitted Himself to be baptised by John. And one very important thing we learn about the life of Jesus is that He was submitted to God the Father on earth until He was received back again to the Father.

God calls us to fulfil our purposes on earth according to what He has already predestined in His wisdom. Romans 8:30, says, "Moreover whom He did predestinate, them He also called: and whom He called, them He also justified, them He also glorified." When Jesus was born His parents were faced with a challenge that Herod was troubled together with all Jerusalem and wanted to kill the child. Therefore they were warned of God to go to Egypt till the death of Herod. And this is very important because Jesus was going to serve God in the land of Israel but at that moment He had to be temporarily taken away from Israel, to Egypt, for His safety. Matthew 2:15, "And was there until the death of Herod: that it might be fulfilled which was spoken of the Lord by the prophet, saying, out of Egypt have I called my Son."

When Marry and Joseph returned, with Jesus, they were afraid to go to Judea because of Archelaus son of Herod who was reigning there. Being warned of God they turned to Galilee. So God Himself was leading them in order to protect what He had caused Marry to conceive. Matthew 2:23, says,

"And he came and dwelt in a city called Nazareth: that it might be fulfilled which was spoken by the prophets, He shall be called a Nazarene." Maybe when Joseph and Marry were going through all these they thought they were just circumstances of their life. But the scriptures above shows that those things were already foretold. If they were foretold it means they were predestined. So then nothing is new to God.

I will close with Isaiah 42:5; it says, "Thus saith God the Lord, He that created the heavens, and stretched them out; He that spread forth the earth, and that which cometh out of it; He that giveth breath unto the people upon it, and spirit to them that walk therein: I the Lord have called thee in righteousness, and will hold thine hand, and will keep thee, and give thee for a covenant of the people, for a light of the Gentiles; To open the blind eyes, to bring out the prisoners from prison, and them that sit in darkness out of the prison house. I am the Lord: that is my name: and my glory will I not give to another, neither my praise to graven images."

Four Very Important Things you need in Order to Make an Impact in Life:

• **Purpose Consciousness**: This has to do with knowing and focusing on the assignment given to you by God. Living authentically.

• **Love and Compassion**: This is about caring for others sincerely as you care for your own self.

• **Knowledge and Wisdom**: Information you possess, that destroys the lies and deception of Satan, and capacity to apply it.

• **Determination**: The will and the readiness to give your best and to go extra mile. Pursuit of purpose with a winning mind.

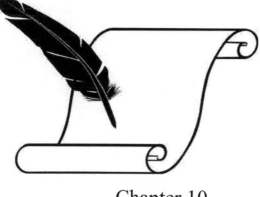

Chapter 10

ATTITUDE

Humility:

Paul to the Philipians 2:3 said, "Let nothing be done through strife or vain glory; but in lowliness of mind let each esteem other better than themselves." This means you must not do anything or serve God with pride, seeking to be seen or known. We do not show forth God's righteousness when we seek to be seen or to be known, but when we seek to make Him known. John the Baptist said, "He must increase, but I must decrease."-John 3:30. This is one of the greatest declarations anyone can ever make. Humility begins when you realise that we are not living to seek vain glory for ourselves but to glorify Jesus; to make Him known and lift up His righteousness. If we have this mind there will be no reason to strife, compete, envy or trying to pull each other down. We will be able to esteem others better than ourselves and God will be glorified.

Philippians 2:5 says, "Let this mind be in you, which was in Christ Jesus: Who being in the form of God, thought it not robbery to be equal with God: But made Himself of no reputation and took upon Him the form of a servant, and was made in the likeness of men: And being obedient unto death even the death of the cross." This shows us that Jesus had a certain mind that we aught to have. He came from glory, with all power, being equal with God, but He willingly humbled Himself, among men, to serve them and was obedient to God and submitted Himself even to die on the cross. That means His awareness of His own greatness did not stop Him from obeying God by serving men who had nothing on their own.

Isaiah 53:7 says, "He was oppressed and He was afflicted, yet he opened not His mouth: He is brought as a lamb to the slaughter and as a sheep before her shearers is dump, so He opened not His mouth." He was oppressed and afflicted not because He had no power over oppression and affliction but so that He could redeem our freedom from oppression and affliction. He willingly gave Himself as a ransom for us. John 10:17 says, "Therefore doth my Father love me, because I lay down my own life, that I might take it again. No man taketh it from me, but I lay it down of myself. I have power to lay it down, and I have power to take it again. This commandment have I received of my Father."

Those who humble themselves before God, for His own pleasure and purpose, are elevated by Him. Isaiah 53:12 says, "Therefore will I divide Him a portion with the great, and He shall divide the spoil with the strong: because He hath poured out His soul unto death; and He bare the sin of many, and made intercession for transgressors." In order to pay for our sins Jesus had to go to the cross, and was crucified with transgressors and He looked like a man condemned together with the sinners, which is why it says "He was numbered with the transgressors." To many who were watching He did not seem better than the two men who were crucified. Probably the same way they thought of many who were crucified before Him is the way they thought of Him.

1 Peter 5:6 says, "Humble yourselves therefore under the mighty hand of God, that He may exalt you in due time: Casting all your care upon Him; for He careth for you." In verse 10 it says, "But God of

all grace, who hath called us unto His eternal glory by Christ Jesus, after that ye have suffered a while, make you perfect, stablish, strengthen, settle you." This shows us that in order to humble ourselves before God we need to be patient with Him because He is patient with us.

Pride is not when you are confident, secure, courageous, bold and focused on your definite chief aim life. If there are some things you choose not to do and some you choose to do, because of something you are aiming at that is not a reflection of pride or arrogance. Pride and arrogance have to do with an attitude of being contemptuous towards others. It is when you look at others and undermine their value and lift up your own value in your own eyes. It is an act of degrading others, and undermining the potential of others because you feel you are greater and higher than them.

It is imperative to understand that everyone has an important role and assignment on earth. If you look at yourself and at others through God's eyes you will see that we all have one thing in common; we are all God's creation. Let me give you an illustration. The sun is the bigger than all the nine planets of our solar system. It is bigger and brighter than the moon. It has its own role and it manifests God's glory in its own way and so does the moon, planets and other stars. The greatness of the sun does not mean the moon and planets have no value or are less important. The sun and all the other celestial bodies are simply God's creation. As a matter of fact the sun profits the earth, but there are many other stars that are bigger and brighter than the sun that we do not see from the earth because they are far away from the earth than the sun is.

Unity:

Unity and peace in the church is indispensable. The Spirit of God himself is the Spirit of unity. In John 17:20, Jesus said, "I do not pray for these alone, but also for those who will believe in Me through their word; that they all may be one, as You, Father, *are* in Me, and I in You; that they also may be one in Us, that the world may believe that You sent Me."

To the Ephesians the apostle Paul wrote, "I, therefore, the prisoner of the Lord, beseech you to walk worthy of the calling with which you were called, with all lowliness and gentleness, with longsuffering, bearing with one another in love, endeavouring to keep the unity of the Spirit in the bond of peace. *There is* one body and one Spirit, just as you were called in one hope of your calling; one Lord, one faith, one baptism; one God and Father of all, who *is* above all, and through all, and in you all."- Ephesians 4:1-6.

In Ephesians 4:11-13, Paul says, "And He Himself gave some *to be* apostles, some prophets, some evangelists, and some pastors and teachers, for the equipping of the saints for the work of ministry, for the edifying of the body of Christ, till we all come to the unity of the faith and of the knowledge of the Son of God" The reason why He has given them is not that they may compete with one another, but to bring the church to the unity of faith and knowledge of Jesus. That is to bring the body of Christ to a place where we do not contradict each other in faith and in knowledge.

Again in 1 Corinthians 3:3-5, the apostle Paul says, "for you are still carnal. For where *there are* envy, strife, and divisions among you, are you not carnal and behaving like *mere* men? For when one says, "I am of Paul," and another, "I *am* of Apollos," are you not carnal?" He carries on in verse 21-23 and says, "Therefore let no one boast in men. For all things are yours: whether Paul or Apollos or Cephas, or the world or life or death, or things present or things to come—all are yours. And you *are* Christ's, and Christ *is* God's."

When satan sees that two or more people standing together are becoming more dangerous to his kingdom he will try to sow a seed of strife between them in order to separate and destroy them. It is like an enemy breaking into your house and injects you and your household with venom that does not kill you but makes you see each other as enemies. He does so, so that you may fight each other. While you fight each other he will be fighting you, trying to destroy the strongest of you. You will spend all the time fighting each other until you have no more strength to fight and until you consume each other and there will be no progress for you. That is why Paul said, "But if you bite and devour one another, beware lest you be consumed by one another!"-Galatians 5:15.

It is like watching a movie in which the main character finally comes face to face with his ultimate enemy. Can you imagine how bad it will be if his own brother or friend comes and start fighting him at that moment and distract him from facing the real enemy? His victory against his brother or friend does not crush the enemy. This happens in many people's lives as a plan of the enemy himself because he knows he can not match the power they have in them.

I remember watching a movie by Schwarzenegger (Terminator 2). The terminator was a robot that was programmed to protect the main character (John Karna) who had a great assignment to fulfil in his life. Towards the end of the movie the programme of the terminator was corrupt and he started fighting against John Karna in stead of protecting him and he almost killed him. That means if the ultimate enemy of John Karna was present at that time it would be easy for him to destroy John Karna. So what the terminator did was to shut himself down. He started hitting the bonnet of a car with both his hands until his cpu switched off. When he rose up the enemy of John Karna had arrived already. The good news is when this terminator rose up his program was reset and he knew that he had to protect John Karna, and not to fight against him. And with the help of the terminator John Karna won.

The spirit of division is a very dangerous spirit. The only way for us to win against it is to reset the programme of our understanding through the word of God. We must refuse to fight the wrong enemy. We must refuse to fight with those we are suppose to stand with. Doing so is wasting time and self sabotage.

Harmony is the music of heaven. And not protecting your divine relationships is a serious error. There are some very important relationships in our lives that we must protect by all means. These are relationships that are meant to help us to get to our destinies. Satan targets these relationships in order to destroy destinies. Our divine relationships are like special boats that have the capacity to bring us to our ultimate destinies. These relationships are above our biological relationships.

Forgiveness:

It is important for everyone on earth to understand that there is nothing God can not do for us and there is nothing he does not want to do for us. He sent Jesus to give us eternal life and to qualify us to receive all His promises in Christ. Among a number of things one of the things that hinder many from seeing the manifestation of what God has given, is unforgiveness. Because of unforgiveness many people block themselves from progressing. They let things that have happened in the past affect their attitude towards the present, which ultimately affect their future. The sorrows and thoughts of the negative events of the past are nothing but burdens that weigh us down and block our hearts from receiving. They stop us from rejoicing and living our lives the way we should today. You can not fly today while carrying burden of yesterday. We must let it go and move on. We must do our best to embrace today without being hindered by what happened yesterday. We can not change the past but we can do our best today to affect tomorrow.

The first most important thing that unforgiveness impacts negatively, is our relationship with God. Jesus said, "If you do not forgive men their trespasses your heavenly father will also not forgive you your trespasses." In order to be able to forgive men we need to depend on God. It is when we embrace His forgiveness towards us that we are able to forgive others their wrongs towards us. Because of His forgiveness we do not owe the devil anything. We do not owe people anything except love and respect. We do not owe the flesh anything. There is nothing good that unforgiveness gives to us. It takes from us and it destroys us. We must be ready to forgive people everyday. We must ask God in prayer to help us to forgive. We must not carry the burdens of pain upon us. We must hand them over to Him. The more we do so the stronger we become and the more we are able to thrive today. We must refuse to hold men in our hearts. We must be conscious that we are on a journey that will end with us seeing the Lord face to face. We do not want see Him holding people in our hearts. We called to live a life of peace and joy in Christ and nothing is worth taking that away. Our joy and our peace are in Him and therefore it is in Him that we find strength to forgive.

Honouring your Spiritual Covering:

Someone who serves as spiritual cover is above teachers and mentors, and has an important role to play in the lives of God's people. Only a true man or woman of God can be assigned and authorised by God as a spiritual cover. Just like every one has a call to answer and an assignment to fulfil on earth so are those who are called to serve as spiritual covering. A child of God who does not acknowledge and honour his spiritual cover is a person who is weak in covenant. Satan can try everything, but there is nothing he can do about covenant. Order in the kingdom of God is designed by God Himself and he saw it fit in His wisdom to set some as spiritual over others. Just as we have the Holy Spirit with his own assignment and angels of different ranks with their different assignments so we have spiritual parents for a reason.

It is important to understand that spiritual parents do not take the place of God in your life, and their relationship with you does not replace your relationship with God. They are simply assigned and commissioned by God to serve His people. In spite of the imperfections of your spiritual parent, when God gives him/her a word or an instruction for you, you must receive and believe it whole heartedly, with a pure heart, as if you were receiving it from God directly. God does not give someone as a spiritual cover because he/she is a perfect person. He/ she is chosen by grace to be the mouth piece of God. As a man/ woman he may have short falls, but that does not mean God is not using him/her.

In Galatians 2:11, Paul said, "Now when Peter had come to Antioch, I withstood him to his face, because he was to be blamed; for before certain men came from James, he would eat with the

Gentiles; but when they came, he withdrew and separated himself, fearing those who were of the circumcision. And the rest of the Jews also played the hypocrite with him, so that even Barnabas was carried away with their hypocrisy." Paul's argument here was that Peter on account of the presence of the Jews conducted himself in a way not aligned with the truth. But this does not mean Peter was not a man of God. In fact two verses before the one above, in Galatians 2:8, Paul says, "for He who worked effectively in Peter for the apostleship to the circumcised also worked effectively in me toward the Gentiles."

Walking in covenant with your spiritual cover opens you to profit from the promises God made to him/her, even in your absence. This is how Aaron walked in covenant with Moses. When the two of them went to meet Pharaoh in Exodus 5:3, they did not say the Lord met with Moses. They said, "The God of the Hebrews hath met with **us**:" Meaning, even if Aaron was not there when God spoke to Moses, he was entitled to declare what God had said to Moses, before Pharaoh.

We must honour our spiritual parents and leaders both in their strengths and in their weakness. We must not honour them based on what they have or do not have in the physical. Paul acknowledged the honour of the Galatians towards him, saying, "And my temptation which was in my flesh ye despised not, nor rejected; but received me as an angel of God, even as Christ Jesus". - Galatians 4:14. Paul didn't say this because he desired their honour but because he knew that that attitude toward him profited them. Somebody once said that, "spiritual protocol is not temporal, it is spiritual" Our relationship with our spiritual parents is spiritual.

A perfect disciple is one who is like his master/ teacher. When one finally gets a hold of what is in the heart of his spiritual father, the burden that keeps him on his knees, he has understood it. Ultimately all this is not about man but God Himself, your creator and the maker of heaven and earth. We must also make sure that we honour not only our own spiritual parents but also the call and the anointing of God in the life of every other man of God else where in the world.

Fearlessness:

Psalm 118:6, says, "The Lord is on my side; I will not fear: what can man do unto me? The Lord taketh part with them that help me: therefore shall I see my desire upon them that hate me." What this verse simply means is that God stands with those that stand with you and is against those that stand against you. Your confidence is that God is on your side, and there is nothing anybody can do to you, except what you let them. It does not matter if someone comes against you in the spirit or in the physical; they will not prosper because God is on your side.

The psalmist in Psalm 27:1, says, "The Lord is my light and my salvation; whom shall I fear?" The Lord is the light that reveals the truth to you. Only a person who does not know the truth is tormented by fear. When you know the truth the way is clear before you. There is no confusion, guessing, or stumbling. There is certainty and confidence. It is the truth God reveals to us by His light that sets us free from fear. And the Lord is your salvation to deliver and save you from all trouble.

Proverbs 3:25, says, "Be not afraid of sudden fear, neither of the desolation of the wicked, when it cometh. For the Lord shall be thy confidence, and shall keep thy foot from being taken." This verse is giving us counsel that we do not need to be afraid because of what happens outside and around us. And the reason for that is that the Lord is our confidence for He keeps us from being taken.

1 John 4:18 says, "There is no fear in love, but perfect love casts out fear: because fear hath torment. He that feareth is not made perfect in love." Only perfect love has power to cast out all fear of anything, present, past and in the future. God is love and love has power over everything. Nothing rules over love. Nothing can prevail over

love. Love is eternal and it conquers all things. In love there is everlasting peace and joy. In love there is freedom and rest. Love sets us free from fear. In verse 19 he says, "We love Him because He first loved us." We walk not looking unto man but unto Jesus who is the author and finisher of our faith. Our confidence is in His love for us and our joy is spreading His love.

Romans 8:9 says, "But ye are not in the flesh but in the spirit, if so be that the spirit of God dwells in you. Now if any man hath not the spirit of Christ he is none of His." If we are in the spirit we can be afraid of evil in the flesh. And if the spirit of Christ be in us we can not be afraid of evil in the spirit.

Don't panic any day, because of anything, for God is always with you. He will never leave you nor forsake you.

Remembering the Lord:

Everything that happens on earth happens for a reason. When God elevates us it is for a purpose. Deuteronomy 8:18, says, "But thou shalt remember the Lord thy God; for it is He that gives thee power to make wealth." That means when we have gotten wealthy we ought to remember the Lord for it is Him who gives us power to get wealth and He has given us the wealth for a purpose. If we forget the Lord who gave us wealth we may fail to fulfil the purpose for which the wealth is given. When God gives us power to get wealth it is simply a fulfilment of His promise according to His covenant.

But the most important question is what does Moses mean when he says, "But thou shalt remember the Lord thy God; for it is He that gives thee power to get wealth;" Part of the answer to this question is in what Moses said to them in the verses before this one. In verse 11, he says, "Beware that thou forget not the Lord thy God, in not keeping His commandments, and His judgements, and His statutes, which I command thee this day." To put the Lord to remembrance is not really carrying on saying the name of God with your lips while your heart is far from Him. So the first counsel Moses gives concerning remembering the Lord is that we must carry on honouring the word of God and holding on to it. No amount of wealth makes the word of God less important. In the word of God is where we find out what is true and what His will is. If we lose the word we lose our way.

I also love what he says in verse 14. He says, "Then thine heart be lifted up, and thou forget the Lord thy God, which brought thee forth out of the land of Egypt, from the house of bondage; Who led thee through the great and terrible wilderness, wherein were fiery serpents, and scorpions, and drought, where there was no water...." This means you must remember the way the Lord has brought you; How

He preserved and kept you strong even when there was no one there for you or to help you. He is the only one who never left or forsook you. Even when no one else understood He did.

In verse 17, he says, "And thou say in thine heart, my power and might of mine hand hath gotten me this wealth." And the second thing is if you will start losing respect for the word of God in your heart, your heart will start deceiving you into thinking that it is because of your potential, skills, knowledge, wisdom, goodness, connections, experience, or because of your own doing that you have gotten wealth. But if you carry on honouring and pursuing the word of God you will in stead grow in wisdom while you grow in wealth. That means you must carry on spending time on the word of God and in prayer. You will constantly be conscious that everything you have is the Lord's and He has given it to you. You must carry on honouring and seeking to obey the voice of the Holy Spirit.

The power that God gives us to make wealth is spiritual. It does not matter whether it starts to manifest through an idea, a phone call, a meeting, a connection, an encounter or a sudden miracle. It is all orchestrated by the Holy Spirit. Without the work of the Holy Spirit it will not be possible. So God gives us this power and carries on working, and making us prosperous from glory to glory.

The other very important thing is that we must be careful of people around us. There are people around us who do not know the word of God, and those who do not respect His word and His ways. They have no regard for what is in the heart of God. They live just according to their own desires and are controlled by what they see, hear and feel. They live trying to get things just to be seen, to please and impress people. They feed on what people say about them and how they view them. Some of them will come up with suggestions for us that contradict the purpose and the will of God of us. They will try to get you to conform to their life style and to follow their ambitious motives. We must by all means not follow the attitudes of these people no matter how close they may be. We must say no to them. Do not let any one make you do something that you do not feel right in your heart about. Even Solomon said to his mother Bathsheba when she was manipulated by Adonijah his brother to ask for Abishag the shunamite to be given him as his wife. The power to overcome their attitudes comes from the Word and the Holy Spirit. We need the Holy Spirit to lead us. He is the secret for effectiveness in our walk. Growing in a relationship with Him is growing in life. No body matters more in our lives than Him.

We must also remember that there is a spirit called mammon that has set itself as a rival of God, claiming the worship of man on earth. He will work overtime to try and get you so busy and so preoccupied that you may spend less time on the word and in prayer. He will try also to set you up using people around and close to you, to influence your life style. And what makes it naturally easy for him is that money attracts the attention of many and it gives many opportunities for you to be busy with many things. If there is something that nothing must interfere with is your time on the word and in prayer. That is where knowledge and wisdom is and that is where power is. No one will have power to align with God without the word and without the power of the Holy Spirit. The secret of a successful Christian life is time spent in the presence of God. We must also make sure that we do not spend more time doing the assignment than we spend with God (On the word and in prayer). Spending time with God is our priority. Mammon will also seek to get you to spend your substance any where else but honouring God. He will try to get you so busy trying to acquire more wealth and material things and to get those things to be of high priority to you than God. He will try to get you moved by your ambitious motives more than you are moved by God. You must seek God to lead you in your investments and you must honour God with the first fruits of your increase.

In Proverbs 3:1, Solomon, says, "My son, forget not my law; but let thine heart keep my commandments: For length of days and long life, and peace shall they add to thee. Let not mercy and truth forsake thee; bind them about thy neck; write them upon the table of thine heart: So shalt thou find favour and good understanding in the sight of man and of God." This is also to emphasize further that your life must be founded on the word of God. You must be principled by the word of God. A man without principles is like a country without a constitution. We must not be swayed like boats by anyone but we must be blameless before men. We must still treat people with a mortal restraint. Verse 9, says, "Honour the Lord with thy substance, and with the fruits of all thine increase." Honouring God with our tithes and offering helps you to walk submitted to God.

The end of the matter is, it is important for us to never forget or forsake what the Lord has taught us.

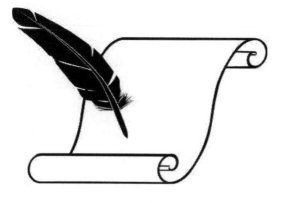

Chapter 11

DOMINION

God the Father, the Son and the Holy Spirit are God and are one. There is no authority and no power above God. The Father has in His great love sent His Son, Jesus, willing to sacrifice Him for the salvation of many. He has elevated Him and put all things under His feet.

1 Corinthians 15:27-28, says, "For He hath put all things under His feet. But when He saith all things are put under Him, it is manifested that He is excepted, which did put all things under Him. And when all things shall be subdued unto Him, then

shall the Son also, Himself be subjected unto Him that put all things under Him that God may be all in all. Revelations 4:2 says, "And immediately I was in the Spirit: and behold, a throne was set in heaven, and one sat on the throne. In chapter5 verse 1, it says, "And I saw in the right of Him that sat on the throne a book written within and on the backside,...." In Revelation 5:6-7, it says, "And I beheld, and, lo, in the midst of the throne and of the four beasts, and in the midst of the elders, stood the Lamb as it had been slain,...." All the scriptures above prove to us that God the Father is seated on the throne with all authority and God the Son, Jesus, is submitted to the authority of the Father.

In Colossians 1:16-19, apostle says, "For by him were all things created, that are in heaven, and that are in earth, visible and invisible, whether they be thrones, or dominions, or principalities, or powers: all things were created by him, and for him: And he is before all things, and by him all things consist. And he is the head of the body, the church: who is the beginning, the firstborn from the dead; that in all things he might have the pre-eminence. For it pleased the Father that in him should all fullness dwell;" Everything that exists in the physical and in the spirit, what we can see and what we can not see was created by Jesus and for Him. Everything is under His feet.

The Holy Spirit on earth has been given authority to glorify Jesus. He has come with three things by which the kingdom of God on earth is established; that is power, love and wisdom. "For God has not given us a spirit of fear, but of power and of love and of a sound mind."- 2 Timothy 1:6-12. Without the Holy Spirit the will of God can not be fulfilled on earth, for it is "not by might nor by power but by My Spirit, says the Lord" – Zechariah 4:6.

We who have received authority from Jesus reign in life, because we are submitted to the power and authority of God. In Luke 10:19, Jesus, said, "Behold, I give you the authority to trample on serpents and scorpions, and over all the power of the enemy, and nothing shall by any means hurt you ." Our authority is not from us; it is given to us by Jesus. It is in Jesus, and it is in the spirit realm which has power over the physical realm. The spirit realm produces the physical realm and the physical realm came from the spirit realm. Faith uses what is in the spirit realm (the Word) to change and create physical realities. When you declare with your mouth the Word that you have come into agreement with then what you say will have power and effect change. Therefore we reign by faith. The church has been given authority to execute the will of God and to glorify Jesus on earth.

Getting Ready for Elevation and Impact:

Many people are seeking elevation and are so anxious for it. They will do anything to go up. The sad news is that many of those people are not ready for it. Some are seeking it with pride and arrogance. Someone once said, "Promotion is not a right we claim; it is a harvest we reap." That means there are some very important things that happen before promotion comes. When you are elevated and have a platform of impact it is for the fulfilment of your purpose and assignment in life. The value of the impact you will make is the same value you give to your assignment. Your assignment on earth is a matter of life and death. Your promotion and elevation is to give you the platform to use the best of your time and potential to do the work of your assignment. It is not for fame or popularity or for opportunity of personal gain. To a lot of people, unfortunately that is what it means. Once you are elevated you need to get busy with the mission of fulfilling your assignment and pursuing your vision. Have clear targets, goals and objectives.

Time of elevation is time to get rid of every distraction and to void every wrong company. If you are too busy with your assignment you will not have time to be occupied by distractions. Let the best part of every one of your days be dedicated to your assignment. When you are serious and busy with your assignment you will be able to see people, who have the heart and mind to help you. Don't spend time with anyone that will pull you back in your assignment. It is not time to join forces with anyone who does not share your vision and passion. Anyone who has an attitude opposite to yours will just be a distraction. That is also not time to have conversations and meetings with people who are full of issues and grudges. These are people the enemy can easily use to mislead/ deceive you; to distract and preoccupy you. Don't be preoccupied by people's dramas. Give them relevant advice and leave it to them. The most effective way to avoid issues and dramas of people is to focus on your assignment.

Don't be bothered by the attacks or accusations of family, friends and even some in the church; carry on focusing on the vision. Jesus was so busy with His assignment that his brothers and mother followed and came looking for him one day. His response to the man who told him they were looking for Him, was, "Whoever shall do the will of my Father which is in heaven, the same is my brother, and sister, and mother."-Matthew 12:50. You must not just entertain any issue. You must choose your battles wisely. You must pay serious attention to what pertains to your purpose and vision and leave the rest. There are people who love to judge others and regard their own judgement final. They will judge you and even hate you if they do not approve of your choices and are not pleased by your decisions. Some will accuse and hate you just because your choices do not favour them or what they are looking forward for. But as for you, be at peace. Thou they may condemn and hate you God is still on your side. Do not fight them. Do not think about their words and actions against you. Progress as if you have seen or have heard nothing. Keep your self away from them lest they pull you down. As long as you have a plan and are focused on it they will not trouble you.

Do not allow people close to you to use your position of elevation or empowerment to punish or cause pain to those they have ever been offended by. Promotion from the Lord is not for repaying evil for evil. Power is not good unless be good he that has it. That means one who is elevated has a serious responsibility of making sure that people close to him understand this. One time the disciples of Jesus were offended by Samaritans who refused to receive Jesus because of religious issues they had with Jews. They asked Jesus if they could command fire to come down and consume them as did Elijah. They even had a scriptural reference for what they were about to do. Luke 9:55, says, "But Jesus turned, and rebuked them, and said, ye know not what manner of spirit you are of. For the son of man is not come to destroy men's lives but to save them." And also, we must not let anyone use us to oppress or walk over someone. Respect everyone and don't let anyone mistreat anyone to impress you. Let no one sacrifice someone else to try and please you.

Every one will be seeking your attention, to be close to you, to spend time with you, to be in good terms with you and to be your friend. Even those who were standing against you before will seek to draw near to you. Don't waste time being distracted by them. Without being apologetic, commit your time on your assignment and to anyone who has the heart, mind, attitude and time to assist you with the fulfilment of the assignment. You must invest your time in what will bring excellent progress to your assignment and in those who will not only do something to help in the present but also in future (Those are people who will carry the vision with you). Some of those people will seek to use you for their own agendas. Some will with many reasons, that are just selfish, seek to make their enemies your enemies. Be principled and refuse to be tossed about like a boat in the sea. Refuse to be impartial, and look at every one through God's eyes. Never ever allow anyone to make a judgement on anyone and give it to you as a verdict against that person. There is only one judge of man, who is God and He will lead you on how to judge every course. Seek only to be on the side of God, because He never loses and he is never wrong. His side is found by fearing Him and not judging any man. Be not a friend of one who is always seeking only their own best interest.

You will be approached by many who will be trying to get something from you. They are always seeking to be recognized and to be elevated by someone. They don't trust God but people for elevation. They will be coming with business plans and concepts/ ideas. Don't focus on such people. Focus on those whose hearts are set to help others. Don't focus on people who are coming to you for material gain. Ask God to lead you and focus on people God Himself is leading you to. When you meet the right people they will not be seeking or fighting to get something. Their priority will be to impact the lives of others. They will not be interested in what you have on the outside but what is in your heart. People who are compassionate about others are the best people for you to focus on. However God's judgement is the best. Usually the right people will not come through your effort or through their own effort but God will cause you to meet them. Such people will love the Lord sincerely and they will love His justice.

Never give anyone an impression that you are going to elevate them. Help them to understand that what they need is not to get something from someone but to get an inheritance from the Lord. Let no one cleave to you/ or favour you for material benefit from you. Refuse unnecessary business meetings. Get busy with the work of the kingdom. Be courageous and don't be afraid to be assertive.

Set priorities, goals and objectives. Define your vision and mission clearly. Spend time in the right company always, even if it means being with one or two people. Your main priority and focus must be God. Be responsible to plan and strategize about your assignment and keep doing so. Spend more time with God and in prayer. The more you focus on the assignment is the more many will speak against you and try to discourage you. Don't worry because your priority is not to make friends, but to fulfil your purpose. Do not ever seek to please people; whoever does so can not please God. People will only manage to manipulate you if you do not have a solid plan that is clear to you.

Many of the people you have known for long will manifest as beneficiaries. Beneficiaries are not your priority. Their own priority with you is just to benefit material things from you. They will not really be there to add value to your purpose and assignment. This may include family and many who are not directly your family. Do not let such people use you or distract you from the purpose. If you let them use you, two things may happen; they may either destroy themselves or pull you down. Don't shut your ears to the Holy Spirit and do not despise or throw away what He has taught you. He is your first true friend, and your senior partner.

Be ready for the envy, jealousy and hatred of man. When the glory of God manifests it shines so bright and some times it attracts the attention of wrong people. Many will persecute you, hate you and seek your down fall because of envy and jealousy. Do not expect every one to celebrate the fact that you are doing something good or glorifying Jesus. Many will look at you like you are trying to be better than them, as if you are doing what you are doing for yourself or for your own glory. Some of those people will be people you have known for long, some will be family and some will be strangers. Don't handle them emotionally but through the counsel of God. When Herod heard of the birth of Jesus He was troubled together will all Jerusalem. He immediately purposed to kill the child; not because the child was evil but because of the potential of greatness in Him. And because of that God told Joseph and Marry to go to Egypt until Herod was dead. There are people who are troubled by the potential of greatness in others and by the manifestation of the same. That is a sign of a spirit of oppression. It wants you to be only average or below and never to fulfil your purpose. To such people you must keep every important thing secret until what God has caused to manifest has matured.

You must carefully protect what God is doing from them.

There are also people who sincerely feel, think and believe that you are not worthy of elevation or promotion; that you do not have the right material for it. They are convinced that you are not worth anything good, especially if it means to be set high. Some of these are people who smile at you and greet you everyday. Some are even family who seem to want the best for you. Once they see you elevated they will develop hatred towards you. There is no good reason for that, except envy and jealousy. Be wise. Do not be apologetic, because most of them will desire to get you to feel bad inside. The issue is not that something has gone wrong but is wrong attitudes. Some of them will seek to use you to elevate themselves. When you are elevated don't allow anyone to selfishly make you feel compelled to favour them, in order for them to go up. Only God has authority to elevate people, because no man is a God over anybody's life. "For promotion cometh neither from the east, nor from the west, nor from the south. But God is the judge: he putteth down one, and setteth up another."-Psalm 75:6. It is important to understand this because; when a person whose heart is not right with God is elevated many lives are going to be negatively affected by it, with a lasting impact. John the Baptist said to the people, "And think not to yourselves, we have Abraham our father: for I say unto you, that God is able of these stones to raise up children unto God." Stones are things we walk on top of, sometimes without even being conscious of them, because they are always under our feet. What John was saying is do not boast in yourselves and refuse to submit to God because of pride. The point is God has power to take something that is nothing in our sight and set it above us.

People who are due for promotion are those who are aligned with greatness according to Jesus' terms. What is greatness? Greatness is not made of something you have on the outside, neither is it given by a position. There are many ways to define greatness. If I was to define greatness I would say it is the potential to impact the lives of others. What are the biblical teachings and principles of greatness? These are the questions we must ask ourselves. Greatness has a colour, by which you can identify it. The colour of it is in the attitude of the heart. The colour of the heart is depicted by the attitude of the person towards everything in life. The attitude of a man towards God, people and the world, depicts the colour of his heart. That is why Jesus said, "but whosoever will be great among you, let him be your minister. And whosoever will be chief among you, let him be your servant."- Matthew 20:26-27. That is why before elevation comes God will take a man through a test to prepare his heart, and to refine his attitude. When a man is ready in his heart God gives him grace that causes him to be elevated.

Once you start making an impact you start to be visible. When you really begin to make an impact, some people will expect you to boast in yourself, and will treat with such an expectation. They will begin to admire you and to focus so much on you, and end up forgetting that you are just a product of God's work. So they end up focusing more on the product and forget the maker of the product. The maker is the one that has made the product in order to make an impact for his own glory and pleasure.

In Job 33:3, Elihu says, "The spirit of the Lord has made me, and the breathe of the Almighty has given me life." In other words he is saying, I am just a product of His. The impact is made for the maker, not the product. It is all about the maker. That is why it is really not necessary for anyone no matter how great what they have done, to present themselves as a perfect being.

When you are elevated you must seek the well being of those that the Lord has committed to you and has assigned you to serve and impact. Those are your main assignment. God is a God of order; He does not assign someone every where. He gives every man a specific main assignment. Pursue absolute excellence in all you do. Have the discipline of ants and the focus of locusts. Aim high like spiders and work hard like conies.

Mammon:

Mammon's number one aim is to seduce many to a place where they will think they don't need God; into thinking all they need is money, and as long as they have money they don't really need God.

Money is useful for a lot of things on earth, in our lives, in our families, in the church and in our nations. But there are places, money have no authority or dominion. Acts 8:18, says, "And when Simon saw that through laying on of the apostles' hands the holy spirit was given he offered them money, saying give me also this power, that on whomsoever I lay hands, he may receive the holy Spirit. But Peter said unto him, thy money perish with thee, because thou hast thought that the gift of God may be purchased with money." The scripture, in 1 Timothy 6:10, teaches us that the love of money is the root of all evil. Money is not evil. It is a medium of exchange that helps us to account on how we use our time, our skills and potential to earn a living. But the love of it is the root of all evil. All evil includes everything that opposes love and faith.

Mammon is the spirit behind all the evil triggered by the love of money. His chief aim is to get the worship and service of people, which is due to God. This is what satan tried to do when he was tempting Jesus. He has his own system which is designed to control finances with the aim of emptying the hands of believers and filling the hands of those who do not honour God, with resources. That is why he said to Jesus, "All this authority I will give You, and their glory; for *this* has been delivered to me, and I give it to whomever I wish. Therefore, if You will worship before me, all will be Yours."- Luke 4:6.

But in Colossians 1:20, Paul says, "and by Him (Jesus) to reconcile all things to Himself, by Him, whether things on earth or things in heaven, having made peace through the blood of His cross." It says He has reconciled all things, not all people. He has reconciled all things to Himself and it is all under His feet.

Chapter 12

MINISTRY

The Ministry of Reconciliation:

Everyone that is born of God and is still here on earth has upon their shoulders the responsibility of reconciling others to God. The truth of the matter is, it is Jesus Himself who reconciles people to Himself through us. He manifests through us in order to reach to those who are lost and save them. 2 Corinthians 5:19-20, says, "that is, that God was in Christ reconciling the world to Himself, not imputing their trespasses to them, and has committed to us the word of reconciliation. Now then, we are ambassadors for Christ, as though God were pleading through us: we implore *you* on Christ's behalf, be reconciled to God."

In the ministry of reconciliation there is no technique exclusive to just one person. There is only three things that are really to be pursued; that is, love, faith and hope. It is all about reaching out to the lost with love, Fellowship with those who are won to build their faith and fill them with hope that is in the love of Christ.

The two very important topics under this subject are, soul winning and discipleship. Both these are all about love. As a new creation you have a new nature; the nature of love. Soul winning is possible when we reach out to people who are born again, with love and wisdom. We do not look at their weaknesses but at the love of God that does not fail.

Discipleship is all about taking care of those who are won, with love. It involves fellowship, loving one another and building each other's faith. Taking care of won souls is not a Sunday activity but an every day exercise. Discipleship helps those who are won to renew their minds. The ministry of reconciliation is all about this scripture; "And Jesus answered him, The first of all the commandments *is*, Hear, O Israel; The Lord our God is one Lord: And thou shalt love the Lord thy God with all thy heart,

and with all thy soul, and with all thy mind, and
with all thy strength: this *is* the first commandment.
And the second *is* like, *namely* this, Thou shalt love
thy neighbour as thyself. There is none other
commandment greater than these." - Mark 12:29-
31.

I want us to study how Jesus Himself through the
power of the Holy Spirit led His own ministry on
earth. The first important thing we see in Him is
submission. He as a child submitted to His own
biological parents, Joseph and Mary. We need to
first submit to God in our own biological
relationships. That is why even Paul in 1 Timothy
3:5 says, "For if a man knows not how to rule his
own house, how shall he take care of the church of
God." He submitted to John to be baptised by him
at the Jordan River. The second thing we notice is
His dependence on the Holy Spirit. No one can ever
succeed in their ministry without depending on the
Holy Spirit. He is the one to show you the way to go.
Straight from water baptism Jesus was lead by the
Holy Spirit to the wilderness. After 40 days He came
back from the wilderness full of the power of the
Holy Spirit.

So the first thing the Spirit lead Jesus to do for His
ministry was to spend time fasting and praying.
That is what comes first; spending time in the
presence of God alone. The second thing He did
was to begin to lay the foundation. Whatever has

no good foundation can not stand. By the Holy
Spirit He was lead to begin to pick disciples who
were going to be people that He will lay the
foundation with. This is extremely crucial for every
leader in the church; being lead by the Spirit to
choose the right people to lay the foundation with.
You can not depend on what you see or hear but on
the Holy Spirit. In doing this Jesus did not follow
favouritism or emotions. He did not just pick His
own brothers at home or His neighbours. He did
not compromise in choosing people to lay the
foundation with. That is why when many who
joined them ultimately chose to go back He did not
force them to stay. This is the reason why His
disciples were submissive, faithful and obedient.
The third thing is Jesus began to lay the foundation
and build His ministry with wisdom.

Wisdom for Ministry:

• Seek the face of God continually and
depend on Him always. Desire to be lead by Him
and to walk with His power.
• Spend more time on the word and in prayer
more than anywhere else.
• Be strong and courageous and pursue faith
in all you do.
• Lead from the forefront; in prayer, in fasting,
in sacrificing, in labouring on the word, in discipline,

in obedience, in love and in reaching out to the people.

- Follow the voice of the Holy Spirit and speak the truth without compromise.
- Give special attention to those with whom you are to lay the foundation. Build them with the word and ask God to empower them with the Holy Spirit and to fill them with wisdom and love. Fellowship with them.
- Emphasize on unity especially among those that labour and serve in your midst.
- Do not accept the person of men but follow God's righteousness.
- Judge no one and seek not to avenge yourself at any time. God will avenge you.
- Do not involve yourself in the issues of others. You have no authority to judge people.
- Do not go anywhere the Holy Spirit tells you not to go and do not do what He tells you not to do.
- Lift up the righteousness of God before men.
- Beware of men. Let them not distract or discourage you. They will be envious, jealous and many will seek to accuse and persecute you. Many will do and say things to try and pull you down. Psalm 35:11.

As a Kingdom Ambassador there are four things you will deal with;

1.   **Spiritual matters**: You will have to cast out devils, break the yoke of the enemy and set the captives free. You will lead the lost to Christ. You will also have to impact people's souls through the word.

2.   **Physical matters**: This will involve physical pain or condition in the body. You will encounter people who are stricken by poverty. These are physical situations that often have spiritual causes and you will have to deal with them in the spiritual and physical level.

3.   **Emotional and Mental issues**: This will involve helping people who are having emotional pain and mental conditions.

4.   **Attitudes**: Encourage the good attitudes wherever you see them; this includes faith, humility, justice, mercy, purity of heart, peace and many more. Depend on the wisdom of God to overcome the negative attitudes.

Above all things as you build see beyond the local church or specific assignment. The church as a body is to be built through love, power and sound mind. These are the three things that the Holy Spirit has given us to build and to impact lives. We must build knowing that the church is a family; it is the family of God. It is a family in which those who were alone in the world without God find a home. Those who can not find help in their biological families or anywhere in the world must be able to find help in

the family of God. We need to seek the justice of
God for all people. If you are not ready to seek the
justice for the weak, the wounded and the
oppressed, you are not ready to be God's friend. Do
not do it to please yourself but God. The desire of
Jesus is to give justice victory.

Good Attitude in Ministry:

Philippians 2:4 says, "Look not every man on his
own things, but every man also on the things of
others. It is extremely important for a man called by
God to touch the lives of others to not be selfish,
and to not only mind his own wellbeing, but the
wellbeing of others as well. When he goes to pray
his priority is to pray for others, not for himself. His
success is in impacting the lives of others. He
desires to see the attention of God on others. This
was the attitude of Moses. This was attitude of the
apostles. Their hearts were purely after what is
pleasing to God not vain ambitions. Acts 18:24 says,
"And a certain Jew named Apollos, born at
Alexandra, an eloquent man and mighty in the
scriptures, came to Ephesus. This man was
instructed in the way of the Lord; and being fervent
in spirit, he spake and taught diligently the things of
the Lord, knowing only the baptism of John. And he
began to speak boldly in the synagogue: whom
when Aquila and Priscilla had heard, they took him
unto them, and expounded unto him the way of

God more perfectly." Aquila and Priscilla were so mindful of the work and the kingdom of God that they did not just look at Apollos or just talk about him. They took him and filled him with the information he was lacking and perfected that which was lacking for the cause of the gospel. It was not because he had something to give to them but for the cause of the gospel.

The Ministry of Angels:

There are angels on earth that are sent on a mission to help the church. Some angels get sent with messages to deliver to the saints. Abraham was visited by three angels sent to go and destroy Sodom Gomorrah. They told Abraham that his wife was going and conceive a child. When Jesus praying, in the garden of Gethsemane, there appeared to Him an angel from heaven, strengthening Him.- Luke 22:43. When Paul was being taken with prisoners to Italy the boat they were in was a strong wind arose against the boat. When they all afraid, Paul stood said, "And now I exhort you to be of good cheer: for there shall be no loss of any man's life among you, but of the ship. For there stood by me this night the angel of God, whose I am, and whom I serve, saying, fear not Paul; thou must be brought before Caesar: and lo, God hath given thee all them that all them that sail with thee."- Acts 27:22.

The angel Gabriel was sent to marry to deliver the message to her that she will conceive and birth a child.-Luke 1:28-31. Daniel had encounters with angels. Ezekiel had experiences with angels. John the revelator had experiences with angels. Jacob had experiences with angels. And many others saints had experiences with angels.

There are also angels that are sent with power to protect and to assist or deliver the saints from trouble. Peter was taken out of prison by an angel. When the angel touched him the chains on his feet and hands fell. As Peter followed him the doors opened by themselves before them.- Acts 12:7-11. When Joshua and Israel were about to go against Jericho, an angel appeared to him with his sword drawn. He told Joshua that he was there as a captain of the Lord's host.- Joshua 5:13-15.

Zechariah said I saw an angel on a red horse, among the myrtle trees, with horses behind him. He asked the angel and said, what are these? The angel said, "These are they whom the Lord has sent to walk to and fro through the earth." And those that the Lord had sent also spoke and said, "We have walked to and fro through the earth, and, behold, all the earth sitteth still, and is at rest."

There are some people who are in the church, but they think that when we talk about angels and having angelic visitations we are being too spiritual.

They think we are becoming too serious if we start talking about angels like that. But we should not think of angels as some beings or creatures that are so far from us that one day when you are lucky you will see one. We need to understand something; we are not in the flesh. We are in the spirit. There is a difference between us and those who are not born of God. We are sited in the heavenly places with Christ. Something big/ serious happened when we received Jesus.

Hebrews 12:22, says, "But ye have come unto mount Zion, and unto the city of the living God, the heavenly Jerusalem, and to an innumerable company of angels. To the general assembly and church of the firstborn, which are written in heaven, and to God the judge of all, and to the spirits of men made perfect. And Jesus the mediator of the new covenant and to the blood of sprinkling that speak better things than the blood of Abel." That is our spiritual environment. That is where we are. It is not where we visit and leave. Our flesh can not be conscious of this. Our flesh bears witness of the physical realities. But our spirits together with the Spirit of God bear witness of spiritual realities. The question is whose testimony do you listen to? The one whose testimony you listen to the most is the one whose testimony you end up believing the most. Romans 8:, says, "We are debtors not to the flesh to live after the flesh." We do not owe the flesh anything. The issue between us and the flesh has been dealt with. Our physical bodies are a limitation to the spirit world. The spiritual reality is that we are together with angels. We are not just with one, two or five. We are in the company of innumerable angels. The place we are in spirit is a glorious place.

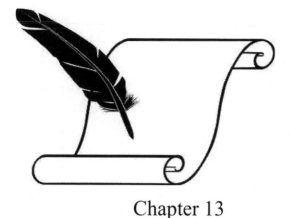

Chapter 13

PROSPERITY

Prosperity is when everything with you is well and flourishing. When you are continually expanding and progressing; when you keep on thriving and going a whole lot further. In other words you begin to fulfil what God has said in genesis. He said, "Be fruitful and multiply, and replenish the earth, and subdue it: and have dominion over the fowl of the air, and over every living thing that moveth upon the earth."- Genesis1:28. You are fruitful in your soul, in your spirit, in your body and in the works of your hands. You see multiplication taking place in your life.

Prosperity comes from God Himself. It is in the power of what comes from His mouth. It is the result of His anointing, favour and blessing upon our heads. Deuteronomy 28:11 says, "And the Lord shall make thee plenteous in goods, in the fruit of thy cattle, and in the fruit of thy ground, in the land which the Lord swore unto thy fathers to give to thee. The Lord shall open unto thee His good treasure, the heaven to give the rain unto thy land in His season, and to bless all the work of thine hand; and though shall not borrow. And the Lord shall make thee the head, and not the tail: and thou shall be above only, and thou shall not be beneath." This means that unless the Lord makes you prosperous there is no prosperity. He makes it happen according to His promises.

When the blessing of God manifests in your life, it does not matter how low you are in life. He is able to take one from the lowest point and set him high above. Job42:12, says, "So the Lord blessed the latter end of Job more than His beginning: for he had fourteen thousand sheep, and six thousand camels, and a thousand yoke oxen and a thousand she donkeys." This is a man who had lost not only all his wealth and businesses but all his children. But by means beyond human effort God gave him all that he had lost as well as ten children.

Psalm 107:35, says, "He turned the wilderness into a standing water and dry ground into watersprings.

There He maketh the hungry to dwell, that they may prepare a city for habitation; and sow the fields and plant vine yards, which may yield fruits of increase. He blesseth them also, so that they are multiplied greatly; and suffereth not their cattle to decrease." This scripture shows us that God by favour prepares an environment to give us opportunities to work with our hands, and He blesses the work of our hands that there may be increase and multiplication.

Isaiah 45:2, says, "I will go before you and make the crooked places straight: I will break in pieces the gates of brass and cut in sunder the bars of iron: And I will give thee the treasures of darkness, and the hidden riches of the secret places, that thou mayest know that I, the Lord, which call thee by name, am the God of Israel." This shows us that we do not prosper because it is just easy, or by coincidence or by chance. God by His favour goes before us intentionally. If He goes before us to prepare the way it means He will destroy every blockage. He will destroy every resistance in the spirit and in the physical. We will open doors that were closed. This scripture also teaches us that God will give us access to treasures and riches that are not given to just any body. He says He will do so, so that we may know He is the God of Israel. That means He will do something anyone and anything they call god can not do.

Jeremiah 33:3, says, "Call on me, and I will answer you and I will show you great and mighty things, which you do not know." That means God is eager and pleased to show us great and mighty things, which we do not know. This manifests and proves His goodness and might before all men. He does not just want to manifest what is common to men. He does not just want to set high but He wants to make us the head.

In Isaiah 54:2, He says, "Enlarge the place of thy tent, and let them stretch forth the curtains of thy habitations: spare not, lengthen thy cords, and strengthen thy stakes. " That means, we are urged to expect more; believe more; See big. We expect from God, not from man and we must not spare our faith and our imagination.

God has through Jesus given us all things pertaining to life and godliness. He has made us the heirs of the world. As He has spoken, so must we confess, that we are blessed when we come in and when we come out. That means we are blessed any time. We are blessed in the field and in the city. That means we are blessed every where. We must acknowledge and be conscious of the blessing of God upon us everywhere and every time. Prosperity belongs to God, and because we are born of Him, it is our birth right as His blessing is.

Satan aims to cause believers to suffer in the natural in order to weaken them and to make them ineffective in manifesting the glory of God. In order for him to achieve this he targets three important areas of life to afflict people in. This is regardless of how much you love and fear God. In fact satan desires to come against those who are more aligned with God, but as long as you are aligned with God he can not win. The Lord boasted of job to satan once, saying, "Hast thou considered my servant Job, that there is none like him in the earth, a perfect and an upright man, one that feareth God, and escheweth evil?"

Satan said to God, "Hast though not made a hedge about him, and about his house, and about all that he hath on every side? Thou hast blessed the work of his hands and his substance is increased in the land." This simply means that satan was unable to access Job, his house and his substance because God had put a hedge around. When you see things going well with you, don't think that it is just happening. You must know it is going well because God is protecting you, and His hand is upon you to cause you to win. That is why we must give thanks to the Lord always.

God said to satan, "behold, all that he hath is in your power."-Job 1:12. The first area of Job's life that satan touched was his business (finances). Job 1:14, says, "And there came a messenger unto Job, and said the oxen were plowing, and the asses feeding beside them: And the Sabeans fell upon them, and took them away; yea, they have slain the servants with the edge of the sword." Job 1:16, says, "while he was yet speaking, there came also another, and said, the fire of God is fallen from heaven, and hath burned up the sheep, and the servants, and consumed them:" The second area he touched was his family. The wind came from the wilderness and hit the house and the house fell on his children. The last area satan touched him was in his health. He smote Job with boils from sole of his feet to the crown of his head.-(Job 1:7). These are the areas that satan targets first; finances, family and health. In order to live in divine health we need to embrace the truth of God, and confess divine health given to us by the stripes of Jesus. We need to also commit our families to the Lord and know that the chastisement of our peace was upon Jesus. We need to lead them in the fear/ honour of the Lord.

The last area of prosperity I want to talk about is the area of financial prosperity. What allows us to prosper and flourish in the area of our finances is giving and focusing on the purpose and vision of God for our lives (Service). There are three men in the bible who I call pioneers when it comes to giving. That is Abraham, David and Solomon. Abraham was not just a great giver of sacrifice and offering to God but he was a generous giver. He was a generous man. We see this in his attitude towards Lot when they were going separate ways. He gave Lot the opportunity to choose first the direction in which he wanted to go. In Genesis 13:9, he said to Lot, "Is not the whole land before thee? Separate thyself, I pray thee, from me: if thou wilt take left hand I will go to the right; or if thou depart to the right hand, then I will go to the left." Hebrews 13:1, says, "Let brotherly love continue. Be not forgetful to entertain strangers: for thereby some have entertained angels unawares." Abraham was such a man.

The other very important thing we see about Abraham's attitude is that he didn't put his trust in money or in people. He didn't lean on people or on money but on the Lord. In Genesis 14:21, it says, "And the king of Sodom said unto Abraham, give me the persons, and take the goods to thyself. And Abraham said to the king of Sodom, I have lift up mine hand unto the Lord, the most high God, the possessor of heaven and earth, that I will not take from a thread even to a shoelatchet, and that I will not take anything that is thine, lest thou shouldest say, I have made Abram rich:" This really shows us that Abraham did not want any man to take the glory of God in his life.

When it comes to giving to the Lord what we learn about David and Solomon is that they were bountiful givers. Wow, that is a good testimony for a father and his son. The reason why they gave bountifully is that they loved the Lord. I believe they loved the Lord so much because they were focused on the love of God towards them. 1 kings 3:3, says, "And Solomon loved the Lord, walking in the statutes of David his father: only he sacrificed and burnt incense in high places. And the king went to Gibeon to sacrifice there; for that was the great high place: a thousand burnt offerings did Solomon offer upon that altar." It was after this giving that the Lord appeared to Solomon and said to him, "Ask what I shall give thee."-1 kings 3:5. Solomon himself in Proverbs 3:9, says, "Honour the Lord with thy substance, and with the first fruits of thine increase: So shall thy barns be filled with plenty, and thy presses shall burst out with new wine."

Lastly in order to prosper with God on earth we must focus on our purpose and vision from God. As long as the burden of the Lord is in your heart He will go before you to make you prosper in all you do. When God calls a man He also promises to walk in covenant with him. He promises to take care of him and to prosper him in all he does and help him to fulfil what he has called him to do. If you will passionately accept the call to serve God by serving others God will elevate you. Mandela was in prison for 27 years. There he was not working to earn a salary or having a chance to save money for the future. If he had a bank account that only he had access to it was closed. When he was in prison many were working and saving money for their future; some were making millions. But when he came out of prison, even millionaires were seeking to see him from all over the world. Not because he was popular or famous. Not because he had more money than them but because of the substance he had inside, that enabled him to impact the world.

Living in the Realm of Prosperity:

There are principles that those who walk in the realm of wealth/ prosperity must uphold:

1.   *They must hate greed and selfishness, and must be generous*. Those who are generous will keep on flourishing and God will increase them more abundantly. They do not follow the way of those who are greedy. They understand that promotion does not from the east, the west or the south. We see their attitude in Genesis 13:8-9, Genesis 14:22, Genesis 45:9-11, Esther 10:3, Daniel 5:17 and Proverbs 15:27. They do not spend time fighting to get material things from others.

2.   *They must have no attachment to material things*. They must have self control and not just spend carelessly. Proverbs 21:20 says, "There is treasure to be desired and oil in the dwelling of the wise: but a foolish man spendeth it up." They must not be controlled or pressurised by what they see.

They must live from inside out. Not from the outside in; not from what they see other people doing. They must also have what we call self determination. They must be able to make decisions free from the influence of people but only the counsel of God who is inside them.

3.   *They must honour God with their substance.* They must honour Him with the first fruits of their increase, with their tithe and with the offering which is more than the tithe. This they must do not as a necessity but cheerfully.

4.   *They must pursue God's love, righteousness (justice), and mercy even more.* These will enable them to glorify Jesus with their wealth even more. They must help the needy and the poor especially those without any help. Psalm 41 says, "Blessed is he considereth the poor, the Lord will deliver him in time of trouble. The Lord will preserve him and keep him alive; and he shall be blessed upon the earth: and thou wilt not deliver him unto the will of his enemies." Proverbs 22:9 says, "He that hath a bountiful eyes shall be blessed; for he giveth of his bread to the poor." This they do not as a necessity but cheerfully.

5.   *They must hate even a hint of sexual immorality.* There are people who when they have a bit of money they fall easily in the trap of sexual immorality. Proverbs 6:32 says, "But whoso committeth adultery with a woman lacketh

understanding: he that doeth it destroyeth his own soul.

6.   *They must not let anyone who loves and respects money more than God make them do things that God does not approve of.*

7.   *Wealth empowers one to help others financially.* The principle is they must not do good for others to be seen by people or to be praised by people. Matthew 6:3 says, "But when thou doest alms let not thy left hand know what thy right hand doeth: that thine alms may be in secret: and thine father which seeth in secret Himself shall reward thee openly.

8.   *They must not worry or fear concerning the future.* They must not worry over something that is not there in the physical. This is the principle of faith. God's favour and anointing manifest more when you are at peace and when you are rejoicing with thanksgiving and with assurance that what they need is already given. Matthew 6:25-34. This attitude helps them to overcome mammon who wants them to worry about needs till they lose peace and faith.

9.   *They must seek to serve God and fulfil their God given assignment with their wealth.*

Starting and Building a Business with Excellence:

Just like it is when you build a house, in order to succeed in business, you must first lay a strong foundation and then carry on building up till you reach the top. Success in the growth of anything you build depends on the strength of the foundation laid. We must be intentional about laying a strong and excellent foundation. So the aim is not just to lay a foundation but to lay one that will be as strong as possible. The more massive the building the stronger the foundation must be. So it is with business. The higher you aim the stronger the foundation you must lay. You need to lay the foundation with knowledge, wisdom, faith, courage, patience, diligence and focus on the vista of where you are going. On that foundation you will then build the walls of your business.

The best foundation in business is laid with God. So the first step is to seek God's counsel and leadership and to depend on Him. The next thing is God will lead you on what to do, where to go and who to do business with and He will connect you with the right people. God is able to do more than all that our efforts can do for us. Proverbs 16:3 says, "Commit thy works unto the Lord, and thy thoughts shall be established." You must pursue God's peace and refuse anxiety. Be calm and confident in God. Sometimes what you need to be ventured into business is one encounter, one door, one opportunity, or one meeting. God is able to divinely orchestrate this. He brings you into divinely orchestrated relationships and sets you on the path of prosperity. You will experience His favour, and His goodness and mercy will follow you in all you do.

People who are ready to lay a good foundation of the journey of success in business are those who with humility are open to learn, are courageous and know exactly where they are going (they can see where they are going). They must take time to research, to learn and to plan. This is a very important process for laying a good foundation of success and must be done diligently. Information helps one to know what to do, to build your confidence and to have effective and profitable conversation with other business people. Secondly they must be able to engage in excellent and professional conversations (both verbal and non verbal). It must be clear in their conversations that they know what they are doing, what they want and where they are going. This knowledge helps one to move with confidence and with conviction and to be optimistic. And also no body will be confident to do business with someone who does not know what he is doing, what he wants and where he is going. When you meet other business people they will be coming with knowledge. The knowledge and determination you bring on the table is what helps them to build confidence in you. However you must never panic and be intimidated in any meeting even if you are meeting someone who has more expertise than you.

In order to be well organised you need to have a clear plan, goals and objectives. You can not be organised and in charge of what you are doing if you do not have a clear and detailed plan. You must be able to communicate your ideas, your plan and the vision for your business, in such a way that those who are listening will begin to see it clearly and believe in it. If it is not convincing and inspiring to you, it will not be convincing and inspiring to them. People do not want to engage themselves in things that are going nowhere. Therefore you must package and present everything concerning your business ideas, vision and plans in a way that they look worthwhile and inspiring. Before anybody can buy into your ideas you must buy into them your self and you must express total confidence in them. Though they may not yet be existing physically you must be able to communicate of them as if they already exist. This is faith. This is what Bill Gates did. He went to sell/ market software that did not yet exist; it was just still an idea. He presented it in such a way that the company he went to, believed in buying it and they asked to be given time before they could buy it. In that time Bill Gates and his friends began to work on the project of creating the software.

Furthermore, as far as branding is concerned you must also brand your own self. Your brand is an image that people have of you. It is what determines how much your presence and interaction with people will impact them. Your brand is made up of your attitude, conduct, communication and dress code. Your attitude must exclude everything negative. It must not pull people down but lift them up. Your conduct and communication must be characterised with confidence and respect. Your dress code must be one that makes you feel the most confident and must be reasonable/ acceptable to those you are meeting. A well balanced brand is one that brings together the best characteristics. People are easily impacted and inspired by a person who is courageous, confident, calm, a visionary, charismatic, trust worthy, fearless, informed and wise, a good listener and someone who can boldly and clearly express his thoughts. The more people are impacted and inspired by you is the more they will love to do business with you.

The other thing is business people believe in making wise investments and are profit minded. They do not look forward to work with people who are greedy and are just seeking to benefit from others. They want to ensure security and growth for themselves. Therefore as you lay the foundation for your own business you need to have the same mind. This will help when you make negotiations. Investors are not interested in how much you need help. They are interested in how their investment in your business will be profitable to them. They want to invest in good business ideas that are pursued by people who have the potential to materialise them with sound wisdom. Therefore you must not seek investment from other businesses for an idea unless you are convinced it is the best and most profitable idea you can pursue at that time and you have the potential to succeed in materialising it.

Once you start engaging in the process of running the business and doing the projects you must focus and work diligently with your hands. Wise business people are focused and are diligent. You must not waste a minute of your work time with unnecessary activities. Proverbs 22:9 says, "Seest thou a man diligent in his business? He shall stand before kings; he shall not stand before mean men." You must put emphasis on efficiency. It is said that excellence is doing ordinary things in an extraordinary way. If you have a team that you work with you can never achieve excellence unless everyone in the team is doing their part to produce excellence. As a leader you will have the responsibility of setting the standard for excellence. Let every one understand the level of quality you aim to achieve and why.

Make sure they understand what is expected of them in their part in order for the collective success to be achieved. They must be excellent in their own role and they must see how their part fits in the whole picture and how important it is. If there are different departments you must find a way to integrate their objectives and goals and marry them to the collective mission and vision of the business. There must be daily, weekly, monthly and yearly targets, objectives, goals, and plans that help to measure the quantity of work done versus the quantity that must be done.

If you will use the best of your potential, skills, abilities, and gifts you will be able to manifest the best of the greatness inside. In order to continuously ensure success you must keep on building capacity and potential for growth.

Planning:

Planning is a very important part for success in business. Planning is a step that helps you to succeed intentionally. Success in anything does not happen accidentally but through a number of steps and choices. Planning is a process of coming up with an organized list of activities, tasks, steps and methods that must be followed in order to reach the goals and objectives for your business. So your plan will show you all that you need, all you have to do, how you have to do it, when to do what and what the expected results are. Through planning you are able to identify the right approach to every activity and to see what will work and what will not work. It is a stage where you prepare for the excellence you desire to achieve. Someone with a plan knows exactly what to do and how to do it. Someone with a plan is organised and confident. A good plan will also help you to be optimistic.

You must Work with your Own Hands:

Proverbs 19:15 says, "Slothfulness casteth into a deep sleep: and an idle soul shall suffer hunger." It is not wisdom to be lazy and it is not prudence to be idle. 1 Thessalonians 4:11 says, "And that ye study to be quiet, and to do your own business, and to work with your own hands as we command you. That ye may walk honestly toward them that are without, and that ye may have lack of nothing." This does not mean you must ignore people. It means when you have work to do you must not waste time talking and disturbing others from their own work. You need to keep a positive attitude and refuse the negative that could affect the release of your potential. You must keep a good attitude towards your work and all your colleagues. Do everything knowing that you are given power by the Holy Spirit to produce excellence that is greater than what is expected of you. This you can achieve through discipline and diligence. To be disciplined in your conduct and to be diligent in your work is wisdom. This helps you walk honestly with those that you work with or work for.

This applies also to the employees in the business or any work environment. They have to submit firstly to those set above them. They need to follow every good instruction given. And they must work with their own hands to achieve excellence in what they are given to do. They must look at every work given as a gift and as an opportunity to use the potential God has given them. They must be able to pursue and manifest their own highest level of excellence without being worried about what others will say or think. Excellence glorifies God and it becomes part of your own personal brand which helps you to be influential. And also every employee must understand that any amount of salary they are receiving is not to make them wealthy. It is a seed. As much as they spend part of what they earn to meet some necessary needs, they need to sow part of it as seed. They must give to God and honour Him with their substance. They must also save a significant amount every month.

Business Wisdom for Kingdom Ambassadors:

• They have a clear vision for their business to follow.

- They see big and nothing is too big for them to see themselves achieving. They aim to achieve things that will impact the lives of many. They refuse to think and see small. They see themselves impacting cities and nations. They see no impossibility.

- They are consistently focused, disciplined and determined, and they work diligently with their own hands every day, with clear goals, targets and objectives.-Proverbs 30:24-28, Proverbs 6:6-11.

- They have courage to use what God has given them to glorify His name. They avail themselves with humility to manifest God's glory through what He has given them. When they do so the name of the Lord is praised and lifted up. That means they know what the Lord has given them and the authority given to them. They seek God's kingdom with all their heart.

- They do not just talk and plan but they put into practice their words and plans.-Proverbs 14:23.

- They approach business with faith and they depend on God to lead them.

- They do business with excellence. They have ability to see beyond what has been achieved already and they have wisdom to pioneer excellence that has not yet been seen. They see big and they set the standard high.

- They communicate the vision, mission and objectives clearly to all those that work for their business, not just once but repeatedly.

- They value and take good care of all their employees in spite of their positions. They believe in the potential of their employees and in empowering them.

- They inspire a culture of focus, discipline, responsibility and hard work among all their employees.

- They are not just found everywhere and they are not distracted by things that do not concern them. They are disciplined and they have self control.

- They have wisdom to expand their business and to take their business beyond the borders of their nation.

- They have rule over their own tongue. They don't slander or speak bad about other people and they don't get themselves in to other people's issues. And they discipline their mouth to utter only the right things. 1 Thessalonians 4:11, proverbs 13:2-3.

- They don't do things with an aim of impressing people and they don't make decisions emotionally but prudently.

- They do not seek wealth through ways that oppose the will and principles of God. Proverbs 13:7; Proverbs 13:11.

- They respect and learn from successful business people who are aligned with God. They keep on learning and growing.

- They do not make commitments that will bind them finically unless they are sure of what they are getting into.

- They do not trust in riches but in the Lord. Psalm 49:10 says, "For he seest that the wise men die, likewise the fool and the brutish person perish, and leave their wealth to others." So wealth should not be seen as a targeted destination. Jesus is our target and in Him is all things we ever need. That is why he promises to give us all that we need.

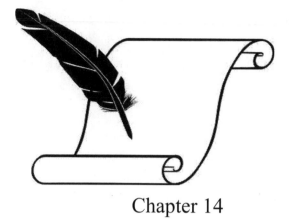

Chapter 14

GRACE AND FAVOUR

On the day Jesus was born the wise men came from the east to worship Him as a king. Straight from there God commanded His parents to go with Him to Egypt for His protection. There are three important things we hear about Jesus as a young boy. Number one is that He knew already with clarity what He was born on earth for. In Luke 2:49, He said to His parents, "…. don't you know that I must be about my father's business." The second thing is that He honoured His parents and was subjected to them.-Luke 2:51. That means before He is seen submitting Himself to be baptised by John He had honoured His parents in the flesh.

The third thing is that He grew in wisdom and in stature, and in favour with God and with man. - Luke 2:52. From there we hear nothing about Him until He comes to the Jordan River to be baptised by John.

After Jesus was baptised by John and endorsed by the Father, He was led by the Spirit to the wilderness, to be tempted by satan. Everybody who heard John saying, "behold the lamb of God", probably hoped to see more of Jesus from that moment on. But the Holy Spirit led Jesus to separate Himself from everybody for 40 days. He was there fasting in the wilderness. In the wilderness Jesus perfectly resisted every temptation from satan. He was indeed a perfect man; tempted at points but still was without sin. When satan left, the angels came and ministered to Him. And coming back from the wilderness Jesus was full of the power of the Holy Spirit. I want to emphasize on the fact that Jesus overcame every temptation of satan because He was perfect. He overcame the lust of the eye, the lust of the flesh and the pride of life because of His perfection.

Jesus went through all these things and overcame, even through the death on the cross, for us. We are not justified because we have overcome every temptation, every lust of eye, of flesh or the pride of life. We are not justified because we have attained perfection of the works, like He did. He overcame for us so that by faith His righteousness may be imputed on us. In fact our faith in Him fulfils all these. He overcame so that He could bring us to a place where the perfect will of God is fulfilled in us. That is why He said cheer up, I have overcome the world. He finished the work so that He could qualify us to receive all the glorious things the Father has promised. We are justified by receiving the word of faith. The word of faith is this; "as many as received Him to them He gave the power to become the sons of God, even to them that believe in His name."- John 1:12. We do not need to search in our flesh to find the reason for our justification. The reason is in the word; in Jesus. Justification is a gift given through Jesus and is received by faith. - Galatians 2:16 says, "Knowing that a man is not justified by the works of the law, but by the faith of Jesus Christ, even we have believed in Jesus Christ that we might be justified by the faith of Christ, and not by the works of the law: for by the works of the law shall no flesh be justified." This is the reason why we can not call a child of God a sinner. To do so is to try and build again the righteousness of works. Faith in Christ justifies us and puts us under grace. Faith gives us access to the grace of God.

To be under the grace is to be in a place where the dew of heaven is constantly falling on you. You receive it by faith and by acknowledging it. It is freely given. That dew is God's favour. It is part of our inheritance, which is received by faith.

Galatians 3:18 says, "For if the inheritance is of the law, it is no more of the promise: but God gave it to Abraham by promise." If we be sons of God there is an inheritance for us from God. Fathers get honour from their children and children get an inheritance from their father. Galatians 3:8 says, "And the scripture, foreseeing that God would justify the heathen through faith, preached before the gospel unto Abraham, saying, in thee shall all nations be blessed. So then they which be of faith are blessed with the believing Abraham." We only ceased being heathen by justification of Christ through faith. And we became sons who are qualified for the blessing released upon Abraham.

Again in Genesis 22:18, the Lord says to Abraham, "And in thy seed shall all the nations of the earth be blessed; because thou hast obeyed my voice." The seed of Abraham is Jesus Christ. This is what the Lord said to Abraham, in Genesis 12:2; "And I will make of thee a great nation, and I will bless thee, and make thy name great, and thou shalt be a blessing: And I will bless them that bless thee, and curse him that curseth thee: and in thee shall all families of the earth be blessed."

In Deuteronomy 28:11, Moses said to the children of Israel, "And the Lord shall make thee plenteous in goods, in the fruit of thy body, and in the fruit of thy cattle, and in the fruit of thy ground, in the land which the Lord swore unto thy fathers to give thee. The Lord shall open unto thee His good treasure, the heaven to give the rain unto thy land in His season, and to bless all the work of thine hand: and thou shalt lend to many nations, and thou shalt not borrow. And the Lord shalt make thee the head, and not the tail: and thou shalt be above only and thou shalt not be beneath:" Everyone of these promises has been given to us who are the children of faith, freely by grace. Jesus has paid the price for all that we need pertaining to life and godliness. He has purchased it all for us in the spirit. Faith is the ticket by which we access the grace which causes all these things to manifest in our lives.

The favour of God upon us bypasses the laws of man and the system of the world. Favour removes all the natural hindrances/ limitations. Where we are suppose to be stopped or delayed because of processes and laws of man, God by favour causes us to pass triumphantly.

The Blessing of the Lord:

Deuteronomy 33:1 says, "And this is the blessing, wherewith Moses the man of God blessed the children of Israel before his death." Moses by God Spirit and Wisdom before he died released to a blessing to each tribe of the children of Israel. Moses was a man equipped to bless the children of Israel because he was anointed to serve as their leader, to lead them in the will of God for them.

The blessing of the Lord is an empowerment/ anointing deposited in your life that empowers you to succeed and triumph in all you do through the favour of God, according to what has been spoken over you. The words that are spoken when the blessing is released are important. In the spirit realm words have power.

It is said that the greatest spiritual gift a man can have is one that has been imparted on him. Elisha received double portion of Elijah's anointing without fasting or praying for it. It was imparted to him when Elijah was taken by God. This anointing was so powerful that it made difficult matters seem so easy. When someone is still alive they still have an opportunity to make an impact. Once someone is gone what we know is that it is over. Elisha died and was buried. Afterwards someone died and was taken to be buried in the same grave where Elisha was buried. When his body touched the bones of Elisha, his spirit came back into his body and he resurrected. What was imparted upon Elisha in one day was resurrected a man when Elisha himself was gone.

When you are blessed you do not succeed because nothing and no one is trying to resist you or stop you. You succeed because the empowerment you have received makes it impossible for anything to stop or hinder you. It is impossible for anyone to curse you or stop you. It does not matter what comes against you and how it comes. What is beautiful is that once God blesses no one can reverse it. Revelations 3:8 says, "...... behold, I have set before thee an open door, and no man can shut it:"

Balam answered a call from Balak to come and curse the children of Israel. The Israelites did not even know this was happening. The angel stood on the way of Balam ready to slay him with the sword and his donkey saw the angel and refused to progress and by the mercies of God the donkey spoke to Balam. In numbers 23:19, this Balam said to Balak, "God is not a man that he should lie; neither the son of man that he should repent: hath he said, and shall he not do it? Or hath he spoken, and shall he not make it good? Behold, I have received commandment to bless: and he hath blessed; and I can not reverse it. He hath not beheld iniquity in Jacob, neither hath he seen perverseness in Israel: the Lord his God is with him, and the shout of a king is among them." God through Jesus has already taken care of our sin by sending Jesus to take our place. He does not take away the blessing because of our wrongs or imperfections. In fact we are aligned and perfect when we lean on the righteousness of Jesus. In numbers 23:8, Balak said, "how shall I curse whom God has not cursed? Or how shall I defy whom God has not defied?" No one can curse one that God has blessed. This means we must renew our minds and align with the truth of God so that we do not stand against our own selves and stop our own blessing. This happens mostly through self condemnation.

In order to receive a blessing and anointing one must desire it earnestly. Secondly you must submit to the person who has it and serve under their anointing or sow into their anointing with the right attitude. The right attitude is a humble heart that fears/ honours God. You must honour the person who carries the anointing you desire and serve God under their anointing with gladness. Elisha honoured Elijah. Joshua honoured Moses. Abraham honoured Melchizedek. Timothy honoured Paul. Just to name a few. The reason why this is very important is because God is generational and relational, especially when it comes to the flow of anointing and blessings. Even what comes by revelation comes to someone who is submitted because if you can not listen to a man in the physical, how would you listen to listen to anything in the Spirit.

Whoever honours and desires the anointing and the blessing of God will receive it. The anointing must be honoured as the one who is used by God to release it is honoured. Jacob, thou he had to flee from home for fear of his brother kept on growing and increasing because he honoured the blessing. The anointing you honour you attract. Once you receive the anointing or the blessing, you are able to manifest it if you acknowledge and honour it.

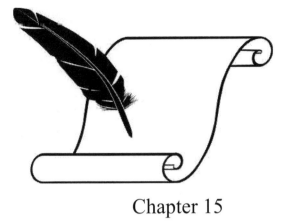

Chapter 15

MANAGING PEOPLE

Wisdom and Love:

We are instructed as children of God to love people, to respect them and to serve God by serving them. But some times because of the attitudes of people it will seem very difficult to do so. We must understand in this regard that our job is not to fix people, but to love, respect and serve God by serving them. We are not even authorised to judge them. To judge them is to expose ourselves to judgement in the same measure. In order to manage people well we need these two qualities;

strength and gentleness. Jesus said be wise as serpents and be harmless as doves.-Matthew 10:16. The type of wisdom He is talking about here is prudence. It means to be cautious, careful, and to be mindful. It has to do with choices and decisions. We achieve this by depending on God and on His guidance. Serpents are strategic when they move and attack. They position themselves strategically and they move strategically. They move in silence and they know how to hide themselves. We would not know how to move and protect ourselves without God's guidance. We must therefore always and acknowledge and honour God and allow Him to lead us- therein is wisdom. Doves are harmless because they do not brace themselves or intend to harm anyone. They fly around peacefully without seeking to bring anyone harm or hurt. That is the attitude we must have. The love of God shared abroad in our hearts and the mind of Christ help us to do this. We must love people and we must honour them with the humility of Christ. That means we do not depend on ourselves to love and honour people. We depend on God.

Jesus in prudence asked His disciples to keep some truth about Him secret until the time was right. It is not everyone that we must expose everything to. There are things that even relatives must not know. We must serve them as Jesus served them. But it is important that we do not allow anyone to try and control our lives. We do not owe anyone anything to be pressurised by them to do things God does not want us to do. We have the obligation to follow what God says, not what people say especially if it is against God's will. It is Jesus who teaches us how to serve people, not those we are serving. Our attitude is influenced by Jesus and by those who are aligned with Him, not by people whose words and actions and attitudes are not aligned with God.

Freedom from Pressure from People when Making Decisions:

As a person you have the right to self determination as long as you are under God's counsel. You should not be made to feel guilty by anyone who wants you to follow their thoughts or opinion or who wants you to do what they think is best. You should depend on God in order to determine what is best to do, without any pressure or influence from anyone. It is your choice to seek counsel from people you believe are suitable, not that someone must just force you to take their advice. In all these you need to be humble and know that a man has nothing by himself apart from God. You must not seek to be accepted by people but to be approved by God. Do not live life trying to please people no matter who they are. If you do so you can not please God and you can not be able to follow His will for you. Make choices and decisions that you know are the best.

If a family member hates you because you did not buy a house where they wanted you to buy, you should not be worried. If they hate you because you married someone they think is not best for you, you should not be troubled by their words, actions and attitudes. You have no obligation to commit to anyone or to be friend with anyone. That means we intentionally pursue peace with everyone but we should keep our lives free from people's attitudes and opinions.

Overcoming Pride and Arrogance:

One of the things you will surely deal with if you seek to make impact in life is the pride and arrogance of men. It is extremely important to make sure you avoid strife caused by the pride of men. Proverbs 22:10 says, "Cast out the scorner, and contention shall go out; yea, strife and reproach will cease." That means if you stay away from contemptuous and arrogant people you will be free from strife. Where you are not able to completely get out of the environment of those who are full of pride and arrogance you need to ask God to help you to handle those who are full of pride and arrogance. A wise person does not rush with words to defend himself, but studies the matter in his heart and allows God to give him the answer of the tongue. Psalm 31:20 says, "Thou shall hide them in the secret of thy presence from the pride of man: thou shalt keep them secretly in a pavilion from the strife of tongues." This is how God protects our hearts and souls from the pride of man.

Dealing with Betrayal:

Psalm 41:9 says, "yea, mine own familiar friend, in whom I trusted, which did eat my bread hath lifted up his head against me. But thou, o Lord, be merciful unto me, and raise me up, that I may requite them. By this I know that thou favourest me in mine integrity and settest me before thy face for ever." This shows that we must not lean on the faithfulness of friends, as they too can betray and stand against us or join those who are against us. But what is important is that in spite of all these, God keep us close to Himself forever. In the shadow of His wings we are safe and strong.

Being Fearless:
Do not ever in life be afraid of anyone or anything. Fear is not of God and it has no profit for you. The fear of man or things is only a snare that causes many to compromise. Do not be afraid of losing the help of anyone. If anyone will withhold their help from you God will send the best help.

Stay Focused:

If someone mistreats you, take you for granted, accuse you, reject you and push you aside, do not hate them. Hating them affects you and it becomes your personal problem. It affects you and your relationship with God. Bless them and leave it in the hand of God. Let them not shake you, trouble you or bother you. Do not spend time meditating on what they think about you, say about you, how they judge you or treat you. Overcome all that through the word of God. Keep your heart pure. The purity of your heart is your treasure. Do not be afraid, do not be troubled and do not hate; it is not worth it. Whatever you do for them do it with a pure heart, knowing you doing it before God. Let them not affect your attitude towards others, negatively. Pursue love, faith and hope. Find courage and strength in the truth of God. John 8:32, says, "Then you shall know the truth and the truth will set you free." Seek the truth, live the truth and share the truth. Before we were all born on earth the truth was there, and when we are gone the truth will still be there.

Focus on yourself, and on what you live for- your purpose on earth. Pursue your assignment and think impact. Invest in yourself and cultivate all that God has given you. Believe in yourself and focus on the love of God. We have limited time to be on earth, for us to live paying attention on anything negative. With faith, we have assurance in ourselves, through Christ and make sure we live each day. If you can love you will live every day. Be secure and do not be afraid of any challenge or opponent in front you, or criticism against you. Do not try to earn security from anything external and do not seek to be affirmed by anyone, for you to be secure.

Helping the Youth:

More than ever before what we see satan doing is to attack the youth with his demonic influences, manipulations and forces. Many of the young people growing up in our generation are quickly taken by the deception that life is all about money and pleasure. They do not get to learn what life is all about and therefore lack a strong foundation for their lives. They do not have a reason to seek God or to seek their purpose in life. It is clear by observation that the information and the knowledge that many of them have is corrupt because it is influenced by satan. The best remedy to this is to teach the young people the ways of God when they are still young. Proverbs 22:6 says, "Teach your child the ways of God when he is still young and when he is grown up he will not depart from it." This is the will of God for every child; that they be taught his ways when they are still young. Without knowing the will of God revealed by the word of God a young person growing will not have a foundation upon which to build a life that glorify God. There is nothing more powerful on earth than the truth of God revealed to men. One of the things that will be a great blessing to every child is to grow up knowing it is important for them to honour their father and mother. Even if they are adopted or are taken care of by someone who is not their biological parents. Ruth attracted the blessing of God to herself because she honoured Naomi, the mother of her late husband. Deuteronomy 5:16 says, "Honour thy father and mother, as the Lord thy God hath commanded thee; that thy days may be prolonged, that it may go well with thee, in the land which the Lord thy God giveth thee."

For those who are already grown and affected severely by many negative things in life it is not too late; there is hope even for them. In God all things are possible. Christ has paid the price so that even those whose life is heading for destruction can find restoration and be built up to live a life that glorifies God. They will need first to be won with love and wisdom. We need to do this understanding that it is the will of God Himself to snatch their souls from the hand of the enemy. So with love and wisdom we need to lead those who are not born again to the Lord. We have to present to them the love and the word of God and the hope found in Christ. Once they are in Christ they need to be inspired, helped and taught to build a foundation for their own lives with God. Proverbs 4:7 says "wisdom is the principal thing." That means the wisdom of God to a young person is a foundation of life. Every young person should receive wisdom that helps him build his own life. Proverbs 14:14 says, "The law of the wise is a fountain of life" That means for a young person to flourish in life he needs wisdom. In proverbs 8:17 wisdom says "if you seek me early you will find me." Naturally when a young person is growing up there are things he or she will start to value and to seek. But the first thing they must seek is wisdom. The scripture above in full says, "wisdom is the principal thing; therefore get wisdom: and with all thy getting get understanding."-Proverbs 4:7.

Proverbs 1:7 says, "the fear of the Lord is the beginning of knowledge: but fools despise wisdom and instruction." Proverbs 8:13 says, "The fear of the Lord is to hate evil: pride, and arrogance, and the evil way, and the forward mouth, do I hate." This scripture helps a young person who has just come to Christ to understand what the will of God is. It helps them to cultivate the nature and attitude of God in themselves. One thing we also need to understand is that many of these young people need healing. They need healing for their souls not only because of the bad things that they might have been through but from the damage that has taken place in their souls. Living in disobedience to God has a negative impact on the soul. That is why many of these young people will live with fear, guilt and condemnation, doubting the love and the will of God for them. Therefore they struggle to find rest in Him. David in psalm 41:4 says, "I said, Lord, be merciful unto me: heal my soul; for I have sinned against thee." In Psalm 23:3 he says, "He restores my soul: He leadeth me in the paths of righteousness for His name's sake." Hebrews 9:13 says, "If the blood of bulls and of goats and the ashes of an heifer sprinkleth the unclean, sanctifieth to the purifying of the flesh: How much more shall the blood of Christ , who through the eternal Spirit offered Himself without spot to God, purge your conscience from the dead works to serve the living God." That means Jesus shared His blood so that we can serve God with a conscience pure from guilt and condemnation. 1 John 1:9 says, "If we confess our sins He is faithful and just to forgive us our sins, and to cleanse us from all unrighteousness."

In 1 John 2:14 John says, ".............. I have written, unto you young men, because ye are strong and the word of God abideth in you and ye have overcome the wicked one." He is speaking to the young men of that church and he says you are strong and the word of God abides in you and you have overcome the evil one. It means they were strong because the word was abiding in them. That means the favour that any young person in Christ can do for himself is to build himself up with the word of God. Studying scriptures and listening to the word consistently will help him to build himself up.

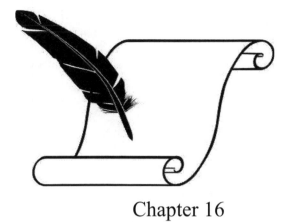

Chapter 16

THE GLORY OF THE CITY OF GOD

John, in Revelations 21:9-27 and 22:1-3, tells us about the city of God. The angel who showed him this city called it "the bride and the lamb's wife".-Reveltions 21:9. This shows us that this city which he saw is the church of Christ, because the church is the bride of Jesus. John says, "And he carried me in the spirit into a great and high mountain, and showed me the great city, the holy Jerusalem, descending out of heaven from God.-Revelations 21:10. The angel took him to a great and high mountain because in order to see clearly the beautiful and perfect work of God one must be elevated to see the bigger picture. That is to be elevated from the limited human mind; to go above human thinking. The other thing is that he saw this city descending out of heaven from God. This is to show that the church is not born on earth but in heaven and it proceeds from God.

According to John this city has the glory of God.- Revealtions 21:11. This means that the church resembles the nature, the beauty and the splendour of God. In Revelations 21:11, he continues and say, "her light was like unto a stone most precious, even like a jasper stone clear as crystal." This is the beauty of the light of the word in the church. The church is washed by the blood of Jesus and sanctified by the truth of God. It shines as Jesus Himself shines.

In Revelations 21:12, he says, "And had a wall great and high, and had twelve gates, and at the gates twelve angels, and names written thereon which are the names of the twelve tribes of the children of Israel." The great and high wall symbolises the greatness and strength God gives to the church through Jesus. Christ is the strength of Church and we can do all things through Him. The twelve gates refer to the governance and rule of God in the church. Twelve angels at the gates, means God has assigned angels with power and authority to fulfil

His will in, with and for the church. They are ever with church. If they are at the gates it means they are able to guard what comes in and what goes out. John saw twelve angels per gate in twelve gates. That means the total was 144 angels. The names of the twelve tribes of Israel in the twelve gates signify the covenant God made with Abraham that He will make him the father of many nations. This destroys the thinking of those who have no regard for, protocol, covenant and submission.

In Revelations 21:14 John says, "And the wall of the city had twelve foundations, and in them the names of the twelve disciples of the Lamb." That means the church is built on the strong foundation of twelve disciples that is laid by Jesus Himself. Ephesians 2:20 says, "Having been built on the foundation of the apostles and prophets, Christ being the corner stone." The angel who spoke to John measured the length, breadth, height, the wall and gates of the city. The length, breadth and height he found to be equal. This symbolises the justice and righteousness of God in the church. The wall he found to be twelve cubits. And the city was twelve thousand furlongs. This signifies God's governance and rule in the church.

John in Revelations 21:18, says, "And the building of the wall of it was jasper: and the city was pure gold, like unto glass.' This just means that the church is full of glory, beauty and splendour. God loved the church so much that he filled it with beauty as He is beautiful. In verse 19, he says the foundations were garnished with precious stones. This is the glory of the word that Jesus committed to His apostles and the perfection them by His Spirit.

John says, "And I saw no temple therein: for the Lord Almighty and the Lamb are the temple of it."- Revelations 21:22. This is what Jesus meant when He said, the time is coming and now is the time, that those that worship will no more worship in the mountain or in Jerusalem but in spirit and in truth. Revelations 21:23, shows us that the spirit and the Word of God illuminates the church. Verses 24- 26, show us that good things will come to the church from the nations.

From Revelations 22:1-3, we conclude that those who are in the church drink of the river of the spirit of God, by whom they bear fruits, through which they impact and heal the nations from the corruption of the system of the world.

This is the glory and the beauty of the church of Christ.

Chapter 17

BUILDING A GOOD SOCIETY WITH GOD

Building a New Family:

In order for a family to begin to be built there must be a leader; one who initiates the building process and gives direction; one who inspires and lays the foundation. The aim must be to build a beautiful family that manifests God's glory. Meaning it must be full of love, peace, joy, righteousness/ justice and power. The people in it must be full of love, peace, joy, justice and power.

They must all experience love, peace, joy, justice and power.

By God's design, the leader and foundation of a family is a man. The aim of the leader must be to lead with excellence. In order to be a good and effective leader a man needs knowledge, wisdom and power. All these three helps a man to walk with strength which is by Christ. A man must be thoroughly built by the word and spirit of God. Therefore in order to build himself up a man must spend time on the word and in prayer. He must seek to fulfil his purpose and to manifest the glory of God everyday. He must be able to live a life that constantly manifests the light of Christ. One of the problems we have in our generation is that there are many men going to the gym to exercise their bodies, than we have those who go into the closet to exercise their spirit.

The next thing the man needs to do is to begin to help the woman God has brought to him to build herself. He must support her and help her to grow in knowledge, in wisdom and to seek the power of God. He must focus on her heart and bless it continuously. He must continuously pray for her to be filled with knowledge, wisdom and power. He must pray for God to strengthen her. He must share with her the truth of God and the word God is edifying him with. Wisdom must be highly valued by the both of them because it is the principal thing.

The husband is God's partner in helping his wife to become the best she was born to be.

The man must have a vision for his own life. The second thing is he must have a vision for his own family. And then he must marry the vision for his life with the vision of his family. In order to build strong walls for their relationship they must have a shared vision and pursue it with one mind. They must do this making sure that God governs and rules their relationship and family. They must constantly seek His will and to be fair/ just towards each other with care and compassion.

They must pursue love and honour. A man loves a woman the best when he focuses on her heart; on taking care of her heart and blessing it. A woman honours a man more when her heart is full of trust in him and when she feels sincerely loved by him.

When the children come they must find an atmosphere and an environment that is overflowing with the river of life. The environment will impact them and cause them to flourish as they grow.

Wisdom for parents:

It is not enough to just be willing to build a good family; you must be equipped with God's wisdom to do so successfully.

We will start with wisdom for a father:

- A father must lead his family with a vision. His vision must involve the impact he wants to make in the life of every member of the family and the impact his family will make in the society.

- He must seek to be the best friend first to his wife, and then to his children.

- He must plan and decide everything with his wife, even concerning the children. They have to make joint force in building the family and in raising children.

- The scripture says your parent is your god. That means a father must by all means follow the example of God as he raises his children. He must seek their best interest and he must lead them with love. He must not abuse or oppress them as God does not lead so.

- He must gently build and teach his children the ways of God when they are still young.

- He must inspire, encourage and uplift every member of his family.

- He must pursue love with all his family members. He must have a large heart to bear with their imperfections. He must cover all of them in prayer. He is the first servant of his family.

- He must support his wife in taking care of the children and must inspire them to love and honour their mother.

- He must provide to his wife and to his children, not only money, but protection and care.

- He must as much as possible spend time with his children. His communication with his children must improve as they grow. He must be involved with their life from stage to stage. He must learn to expressly love the good things they love.

- He must be the first couch for his children. They must gain wisdom form him.

- He must be there to support and strengthen his children. He must listen to them and communicate respectfully with them. When they are lost he must with wisdom and love help them find their way. They must feel free to talk to him.

Wisdom for a mother:

- She must with humility support her husband in building the family and in pursuing their vision.

- She must be gracious and patient in how she deals with her husband and children. She must pray for them. She is the second servant of the family.

- She must support her husband in teaching their children the ways of God.

- She must with love seek to be the best friend to her husband and children.

- She must inspire her children to love and honour their father.

- She must be able to balance between the attention she gives to her husband and the attention she gives to the children.

- She must as much as possible spend time with her children. Her communication with her children must improve as they grow. She must be involved with their lives from stage to stage. One of the easiest ways to bond with your children is to learn to expressly love the good things they love.

- She must be the first adviser of her children. They must gain wisdom from her.

- She must be there to support and strengthen her children. She must listen to them and communicate respectfully with them. When they are going through challenges they must find comfort in her. They must feel free to talk to her.

Courtship:

The purpose of courtship should be to lay a good foundation for marriage and for a new family. People must not date just because they are bored or they need some company. When they go into dating their desire should be to get married to one another. They should therefore lay a foundation of excellence through the wisdom of God. If the foundation be strong and excellent, the marriage will thrive in spite of any challenge. Before thinking about getting married a man must know clearly what his vision for his life is. And he must already be embarking on the journey to fulfil it.

Before choosing a life partner every man has to understand that a woman has an undeniably important role to play in the life of a man in her life. In Genesis 3:17, God said to Adam, "Because thou hast hearkened unto the voice of thy wife, and hast eaten of the tree, of which I commanded thee, saying, Thou shalt not eat of it: cursed is the ground for thy sake; in sorrow shalt thou eat of it all the days of thy life;" That means it is the voice of Eve that managed to get Adam to disobey God. Eve gave hid to the voice of satan, and it was her voice that mislead Adam her husband. Therefore as a man you need to choose a woman who is attentive to the voice of God.
It is also important to understand that such a woman can only be sent into a man's life by God.

Only God can help you conceive and birth a relationship that will give God glory and empower you to glorify God.

Every woman needs a man who is purpose driven; one who has discovered his purpose, which becomes his vision. A man who does not know his purpose will seek to find meaning for life from things outside and around. He is prone to be distracted by a lot of things in life. A man who has a clear vision and aim, for his life, is focused and able to live with authenticity and honesty with himself. You need as a woman to follow a man who has submitted his will, plans, ambitions, desires, dreams and goals to the authority of God. That is a man who will be faithful to God and to you.

The scripture says two can not walk together unless they agree.-(Amos 3:3). Therefore, a man and woman who start dating with the aim of getting married must share the same faith and they must complement each other with their characters, personalities and be able to at least have a common destiny image. While they lay this foundation he must learn to love and lead her properly and she must learn to honour and follow him properly. Their greatest motive should be to lay the strongest foundation they possibly can for their marriage. Courtship is a friendship that becomes the best friendship as you enter into marriage.

Two very important things without which any couple can build their relationship successfully are, love and honour. Both these begin with yourself. You can not expect someone else to love you and respect you if you do not love and respect yourself. You can love and respect someone as you should if you do not love and respect yourself.

During courtship the man's focus must not be on the woman's body and her focus must not be on his possessions. He must seek to sow well in her heart; to bless her heart and to love her whole heartedly. The woman on the other hand must not spend time focusing on the material things he has or does not have. She must focus on his heart and seek to know his heart. She must respect him and learn to support him in his work and in his vision. This is where they begin to learn to be friends and to carry each other's burdens.

They must both take time to seek knowledge from God on how to build a good relationship, marriage and family. They can acquire knowledge from the bible and from Christian books and television programs that talk about relationships. They will also be able to get this knowledge from God through prayer. Haggai 1:8 says, "Go up to the mountain, and bring wood, and build the house; and I will take pleasure in it, and I will be glorified, saith the Lord." In the same way we need to go the mountain (the presence of the Lord through prayer), bring the wood (get knowledge) and build the house (build our lives/ relationships). And the Lord will take pleasure in us and be glorified. In Proverbs 8:14 the Lord says, "Counsel is mine, and sound wisdom: I am understanding; I have strength." We all need counsel, sound wisdom and strength that wisdom gives in order to build our relationships.

Those in courtship must share the knowledge God is giving them and they must talk about their future. They must pray for their relationship and for each other. They must pray for each other's faith and strength. They must pray for one another to be filled with wisdom. Wisdom is the principal thing and they need it to build.

A good marriage:

A marriage is an institution into which those that enter come into a covenant with each other. A good marriage is one that is governed by God Himself or is handled according to the principles of God. There are three important things that every married believer need to take care of in order to lead a good marriage and a successful life:

• The first thing is their relationship with God. That is the first most important relationship and it deserves every believer's best attention and diligence. In fact it is through our relationship with God that we are able to successfully relate with others and fulfil our assignments on earth. They must not seek to excel in their marriages and every other thing and neglect their relationship with God. It is also important to note that by your relationship with God I am not referring to the activities and sacrifices of fulfilling the assignment. I am referring to your intimacy with God, the time you spend on His word and in prayer; hearing and aligning with His voice.

• The second thing is their relationship with their spouse. The relationship between a husband and wife is so important because it is a foundation of a good family. A faulty marriage can result in a dysfunctional family. A group of dysfunctional families can result in a broken community. Broken communities can wreck nation. And also a broken relationship between husband and wife can affect the fulfilment of both their purposes. Therefore it is important not to be consumed by the passion to fulfil the assignment while neglecting your relationship with God and your marriage.

• The third thing is the assignment from the Lord. Our visions, purpose and assignments from the Lord are the reasons for our existence and it is through them that we glorify God with our lives. If you take good care of your relationship with God and your marriage then it will be very easy to fulfil your assignment, purpose and vision.

There are three things that are necessary in order to build a good marriage:

• The first is love. Every man and woman who is married is suppose to love their spouse the best before they try to love any body else out there. They are suppose to encounter love from each other first. In love they must gladly serve each other and carry each other's burdens. They must pray for each other daily. They must share gifts with each other; it does not have to be expensive things but things that are meaningful to them.

• The second thing is honour. They must always listen to each other, and respect each other's words, requests and desires. They must be faithful to each other.

• The third thing is friendship. They must be open, honest and transparent with each other and there must be mutual complete trust. They must spend time with each other more than they do with any body else. They must believe in each other's potentials and encourage each other to be the best they can be. They must be helpful to each other. They must be able to pour out their hearts to each other and give each other good advice.

Over and above everything they must depend on God in order to treat each other well. And they must pray for each other to continuously be filled with strength and wisdom.

Private success in marriage:

Public success with private failure in relationship seems like success but it is failure. 1 Peter 3:7 says, "Like wise, ye husbands, dwell with them according to knowledge, giving honour unto the wife, as unto the weaker vessel and as being heirs together of the grace of life; that your prayers be not hindered." That means God wants husbands to live with their wives and treat them with knowledge. They must apply knowledge from God, and that is called wisdom. Thou they may seem strong He says they are the weaker vessels. They need to be treated with care. To achieve this, husbands need to treat their wives with honour and gentleness of heart. With gentleness they must speak hope to their wives. They must never angrily accuse or blame their wives of anything. With love and wisdom they must help their wives protect their souls from whatever could affect their conscience negatively. They must gently teach and encourage their wives to build up their faith and to draw near to God in prayer. With love they must help their wives to purify their hearts always. As the husband will do this the wife will be able to give back the same to him and she will value him as a person and love him sincerely. This will please God and glorify His name.

The beauty of Love:

True love focuses on giving the best, and not just on receiving. That is what God did. He gave us His best so that He could justify us through His own gift. He made us the best by giving His best. By His perfect gift He tuned us from perfect wretchedness to perfect righteousness. Love breathes life where there is death. Love makes what was dirty to shine. Love embraces and restores. The work of love is the greatest. You have not seen what love can do until it manifests in a place where there is complete hopelessness. The way of love may seem tough but the reward is excellent above all.

Love qualifies the unqualified. It is because of love that though our sins were red as crimson, we were made as white as snow. Love forgives and forgets. In love peace, joy and righteousness are freely given. Love does not follow the way of those who accuse, judge and condemn others. Love shows the way. Love comforts and strengthens. There is no law in heaven or in earth that is against love. Love shines in darkness and makes the impossible possible. In love is all truth and complete confidence.

Love is deeper than all depths and higher than all heights. Love is a house in which perfection resides. Love is the eternal song of the universe. Love is the beginning and it is the end, and it is the way. Love believes the unbelievable and it sees the invisible. Love is the best teacher and leader. Love frees. Love is the river and we are all together like a tiny stone dropped therein. True Love is what Jesus has taught us through His life on earth. And Love is the way we all must choose. Love is full of mercy. Love seeks the perfect will of God for everyone. To love someone is to value their heart (their spirit) and their soul (their uniqueness/ their personality), and to consider their blood precious in your sight (to value their life in the flesh), in spite of their weaknesses and how imperfect they are. It is the ability to reach to someone's heart and see beyond the physical, and beyond imperfections.

Building a Nation:

The goodness of the state of any nation and society begins with the leaders of it. Therefore, it is a great privilege to have leaders that are after the heart of God in our society. When God wants to restore or build a society He will raise leaders that are aligned with His heart. An example of such leaders is king David, one of the kings of Israel.

In order to begin talking about the qualities of a good leader let me share some words from King David himself. In 2 Samuel 23:1 David says, "Now these be the last words of David. David the son of Jesse said, and the man who was raised up on high, the anointed of the God of Jacob, and the sweet psalmist of Israel, said, The Spirit of the LORD spoke by me, and his word was in my tongue. The God of Israel said, the Rock of Israel spoke to me; **He that rules over men must be just, ruling in the fear of God. And he shall be as the light of the morning, when the sun rises, even a morning without clouds; as the tender grass springing out of the earth by clear shining after rain."**

Solomon in proverbs 16:12 says, "It is abomination to kings to commit wickedness: for the throne is established by righteousness." The word "kings" in this case represent anyone that rules over men. He says it is abomination for one that rules over men to commit wickedness. It is totally horrible for them to commit wickedness (to do what is evil). Solomon adds and says, "for the throne is established by righteousness." Righteousness here refers to God's kind of justice and fairness towards everyone. They must seek God's justice and fairness. This is inspired by sincere care, love and respect for the people. This is what will inspire leaders to lay a good foundation of at leadership level for nation building. These are leaders who have the best interest of people at heart. Their hearts are pure towards the people. They seek the well being of people in the fear of the Lord. It is a primary requirement that everyone who leads a nation, his heart be inhabited with sincere love.

There are a number of things that are necessary in order to build a nation successfully:

•	The leader of a nation must love justice and lead in the fear of the Lord.

•	He must be wise and he must not accept any man's person.

•	He must be focused, disciplined, principled, diligent and he must never compromise.

•	He must have a clear competent ethical policy that he fairly enforces on all his leaders and those under them. Commitment to the policies must be monitored.

•	He must be ready and willing to sacrifice himself for others, not others for himself.

•	The team he appoints to work with him must be made of people who are faithful and reliable; people who care sincerely for people.

•	He must be able to make the vision, mission, and objectives of his government clear to all those working under him.

•	Greed and selfishness must be utterly condemned in his team.

•	All those in leadership positions must continually account to the main leader and must be assisted to improve where necessary.

- The main leader must be aware of what is happening in every part of the land and attend to all urgent issues according to the order of priority.

- The care of people must be the priority and passion of every leader.

- The main leader must be able to inspire those under him, to be committed, selfless, disciplined, principled, responsible, accountable, and faithful.

- All leaders must be trained well.

- There must be a thorough process of accountability on every project and task assigned.

- Those in leadership together with all those under them must work in unity and make a joint force for good.

- All those serving the nation must care not only about the current generation but about the next generations.

One of the very important roles you play as a leader is that of being an example and an inspiration. This is allows you to combat and counteract negative influence and attitudes.

There are four virtues that enable a leader to influence and inspire others with a great aura:

1. **Faith**: Seeing and confessing with confidence and boldness what has not yet physically manifested.

2. **Love**: Seeing and thinking beyond yourself; reaching out compassionately to others.

3. **Wisdom**: Being aligned with the heart, the mind and the truth of God in your choices and decisions; seeing beyond the current.

4. **Courage**: Being afraid of nothing. The readiness to face anything and any opponent, and win, without any fear. The readiness to do something that many are afraid to do, without any fear. The motivation to be courageous is not invitation to act irresponsibly. If you find someone disrespecting everyone and dishonouring God, do not applaud for them. That is not courage, but immaturity. Courage has nothing to do with pride, arrogance and insensitivity.

5. **Humility**: The ability and will to go down and be a blessing to others. The will to use the power and potential in you to serve others. Humility also has to do with submitting yourself to the will of God in spite of how bad or good things around you may be.

What allows a leader to be able to make the impact he has to make, is not how well he speaks, how bold he is in his speeches, or how much information he has on any subject. What he needs primarily is to be honest with himself and with others. He can not be able to effect the necessary change or maintain a good state in society without being honest with himself and with others.

There are three things that the former president of South Africa, Nelson Mandela, advised the leaders of a nation to pursue. That is; **a growing economy, full employment and a caring society**. In order to keep the economy growing the country must follow a culture of saving. This culture must be instilled in families, communities, municipalities, departments, and at national level, and it must be regulated as much as possible. There must a certain percentage saved every year. This money must not be consumed or used to cover expenses of the country but must be invested in initiatives that will profit the country economically. The leaders must continually identify profitable investment opportunities and finance them. In order to ensure full employment we must endeavour to equip people with skills. The aim should not be to just give people skills, but to offer them skills and education that will empower them to face the challenges of our time and solve the problems at hand. We need to have a competent education system and have highly skilled trainers and teachers to train and teach our people. Young people must be encouraged to pursue education and the country must make a serious financial investment on education.

The last thing is that we must have a caring society. No one, especially those who are growing up in extremely cruel environments should be lost alone in the nation. There are many young and old people are crippled by abuse and oppression of all kinds', right in our society. Our country must be able to take care of those people. That is the reason why the government is represented at every level of the society. Just as David took care Mephibosheth, son of Jonathan, who was crippled, we should also be able to fairly take care of those who are afflicted and oppressed in our country.

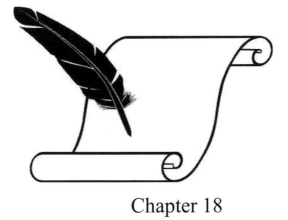

Chapter 18

WISDOM REFLECTIONS

B e not a friend of one who refuses to let go of anger, wrath and unforgiveness, lest you be filled with his ways.

Watch these three things: The deception of wrong friendships; the deception of riches (where riches are seen as a destination); and the deception of pride and high mindedness.

Don't let your life pass you by while you are stuck in the past, because of the wrong someone has done to you yesterday. There is no time to spend mourning over the past.

Time spent worrying in the day or in the night is time spent punishing one self.

Unbelief makes a person to complain about the past, even when they are suppose to be praising for the present and the future.

The most important time in your life today is today because it will determine tomorrow. How you spend it is up to you.

Those who are only focused on personal gain judge unfairly.

A man who is greedy is a friend of whoever he can use to profit himself.

Sometimes when you are more concerned about a certain problem than every body else, it is because you are carrying the solution for it.

There is no progress when you are focusing your mind on the wrong thing.

God trusts you more when He sees that you refuse to be influenced by people against His will.

Many people respect people because of what they have and they undermine people because of what they don't have; before God, that is all foolishness and faithlessness.

A simple thing as living to please God and not people is great wisdom.

There are three important things in life; faith, patience and gratitude.

You must reach this conclusion in your life, that God is above all things and if you follow Him, you will fulfil your purpose on earth.

It is difficult for a man who is discouraged to focus. Find strength in the wisdom of God.

People are not angels. They can change or disappoint you unexpectedly, any time. But the Lord never changes.

A good friend is one who has submitted his personal ambitions, desires, will, plans and goals to the will of God.

Many who have been abused are very harsh. Many who have not suffered, lack wisdom. One, who has suffered many things and yet is kind, is hard to find.

There are people who love to see your downfall. They feed from your weakness. They will not rejoice at your elevation. In the midst of all these, keep your focus on the love of the Lord.

One who seeks peace will always find good.

The wicked sees a wounded man and seeks to finish him. But the wise will help him stand.

When you marry someone what you are actually marrying is their heart. We do not marry for image but for purpose.

Many people draw near to someone for what will profit them. Once what is attracting them is gone they also start looking for a way out. Those are not friends and they add no value.

Speak to yourself through the wisdom of God and be strengthened.

A wise person separates himself from the greed, selfishness and corruption of those who do not fear God.

To stay away from the house of the proud and from their company is a blessing to your soul.

The support of a good friend helps a man to focus and to prosper.

Through favour someone can deceive you, but a friend who fears the Lord is to be cherished.

It is the favour of God that changes the course of a man's life for good, and cause him to be elevated.

Limiting one's vision and thinking small does not help a man to fulfil his purpose.

Don't try to explain what you do not understand; withhold your comment when you do not know.

Don't doubt yourself; what you carry is the best because there is only one you. You were not designed to compete but to give what you have received.

A wise man reigns through the Word of God.

Life does not begin and end with man. It begins and ends with God.

Never stop speaking words of faith into your life and the lives of others. That is your true labour bringing change.

By the fruit of the lips a man is exalted.

Hopelessness weakens faith and steals away joy.

When people hate you and are jealous of you because of the manifestation of God's power in your life don't worry because you are not going forward with them but with God. Take no time to consider issues and let them not bother you.

Live your life building capacity and character for growth and increase. Keep focusing on purpose, assignment and impact. Focus also on what God has given you and make the most of it.

When God starts moving away the help of man from you it is because He is about to do something new.

Sometimes all that is required is one encounter, one meeting, one conversation, one door for you to step into your destiny, to manifest your purpose and begin to fulfil your assignment.

Don't be involved in the issues between friends or siblings, lest you be ashamed when they get together against you.

Thou you hate a man's ways don't hate him. Never use your energy to strive with anyone.

Don't take the word of God out of context or try to use human wisdom to explain it.

Don't receive counsel from someone whose priorities are different from yours, especially if he is not aligned with God.

Here is the end of the matter. Unbelief is sin and is all unrighteousness. No one no matter how accepted by people can please God without faith.

To walk in the spirit is to walk by faith.

Do not respect the person of any man no matter how rich, how educated and how influential they are. Therein is wisdom.

One, who compromises some principles based on who he is dealing with, is given to accept the persons of people. He is deceptive and manipulative.

Speak not to please yourself but God.

Seek the truth, live the truth and share the truth.

Don't seek to be affirmed by people but to be approved by God.

A wise person does not rush with words to defend himself, but studies the matter in his heart and allows God to give him the answer of the tongue.

If you see a rich man who oppresses his neighbour you should know, there is more hope for his neighbour than for him.

If you do not have a vision you don't know why you live.

Honour someone with your heart and not just with feigned actions and words.

When the wicked says something good, take what they say, but do not follow their ways.

Don't be deceived by the smiles and the applause. Some will clap for you but in their heart hating you. They smile before you, but speak evil behind you.

There are people who destroy others both with actions and with words. One who does not respect their presence is wise.

Neither the accused nor the accuser is right, but the one who reveals the righteousness of Jesus.

A man is not accepted by God because he is perfect but because he has faith in God.

When you have faced and overcome so much pain you are able to stand and say, I have seen so much trouble to be troubled by what any body says or does.

Let people encounter Jesus through you.

Don't take anyone's bad attitude too seriously to start striving with them.

"Thou shall hide them in the secret of thy presence from the pride of man: thou shalt keep them secretly in a pavilion from the strife of tongues".- psalm 31:20; This is how God protects our hearts and souls from the pride of man.

To go out of the earth is not a tragedy as long as you have fulfilled all your life's assignment.

Whoever hates pride is satan's enemy and God's friend.

When I succeed on earth I do not succeed for myself or my family, but for Jesus.

Everything you ask God according to His will He has already answered yes, because His word is yes and amen.

You can not help anyone to overcome oppression if you yourself still allow yourself to be oppressed. You can not successfully help someone to be free when you yourself are still not free.

Someone who is dependant will be affected by the attitudes of those he is depending on, and he will find it difficult to influence them.

A wise man is a heavy challenge to one who lacks wisdom.

When God does a miracle in your life some people will refuse to accept that it is the hand of God doing it, because they don't want to acknowledge the manifestation of God's righteousness. Also because, they hate to know that God has favoured you and has chosen to help you. They love to see you forsaken.

Through a number of tests a person grows, matures and sometimes changes in attitude and in perception.

Being in the perfect place with the wrong person is worse than being in the worst place with the right person.

There are problems you will avoid in your life by just making the right choices.

With the proud is disrespect even when you seek peace with him.

When the season has come for something to happen according to God's will nothing can stop it.

Acknowledge the good in you in Christ without seeking the affirmation of people. Believe in what you possess.

Courage allows a man not only to free himself but others.

Appreciate and celebrate what you have received from the Lord. Protect it and take good care of it. Use it to profit Him.

Not respecting yourself means not respecting what God has created you for. You must respect yourself enough to separate yourself from anything that destroys you.

If you have not yet been slandered or hated or persecuted, without cause, you have not yet made impact. For the record, wise people don't gossip, or slander or persecute others, even if you force them or give them a reason.

Give thanks to God always and let not anything intimidate you.

For a few pieces of silver a man's life can cease being precious and valuable in the eyes of his own friends.

The hatred of man against the simple is like deep waters; like overflowing floods.

Life is too broad. Don't spend your time focusing your energy on hating someone or keeping grudges.

When you enter a season of elevation there will be relational shifts and positional shifts.

Your excellence in small things will impact your excellence in big things. Your recklessness in small things will negatively impact your excellence in big things.

Your lasting excellence in public depends on your consistent diligence in private.

Sometimes the enemies of a man's assignment and destiny are friends and family. Therefore make destiny impacting decisions with God and in prayer.

Strengthen yourself daily to say no when God says no, and to say yes when He says yes.

Get up to the mountain; lift up your eyes to the hills and see beyond the river.

Do not laugh about what the proud laugh about. Take seriously what they take lightly.

You have not spent your day excellently unless you have used your time wisely.

Someone who is not living right can not perceive what is good and what is bad.

When elevation and promotion come do not be overexcited. Exercise self control with wisdom. Often when a man gets overexcited wisdom jump out the window.

Expect the blessing of God to manifest in your life daily.

One who is conscious that our time on earth is limited is instructed to live wisely.

A good man sees the best also in others, and not just in himself.

Evil in some lives began in their own families, but I have come to know that the Lord is good, merciful, gracious, loving and righteous. He crowns His own with favour.

Unless I was afflicted I probably could have not known God's righteousness as I do.

Let those of like high minds beg and flatter each other; as for you put all your trust in the Lord and not in the help of man.

Never allow anyone to despise and walk over someone else just to impress and please you.

Do not join those who judge and condemn others. There is only one judge of man and it is God almighty.

In love there is no struggle unless there is pretence.

The greatest thing about love is when you look back and realise that the one who loves you is still there to care always and forever, in spite of the battles of today and yesterday.

Some times even those who seem so close to God, smiling as if they have everything together, can be the worst friends you can have.

Show no respect to the attitude of one who hates, undermines and oppresses others.

Those who do not fear God are hopeless even in their success.

If you help a wicked person to pull someone down, tomorrow someone else will help him to pull you down.

Don't be flattered and don't flatter anyone. Do not accept the person of any one; friend, family or stranger. Don't be a friend of one who is unjust and shows no mercy.

Anytime you take a stand against evil in your life, it does not only profit you but many other people.

Mistakes are forgivable if we acknowledge them. If anyone refuses to acknowledge his mistakes and wrongs, don't fight with him. Give him advice and leave. He will learn in time.

Don't live your life on earth as if there is no end. Our bodies are the houses of our pilgrimage. And everything we see with our physical eyes has an end.

Pride destroys a man way before satan comes to destroy him.

What the proud lack the most is worth more than gold.

Do not give respect to things that God does not give respect. Don't give thought of what He doesn't give thought of. All that God gives respect to in you is your faith and love and the fruits thereof.

Where you are not valued you are given the last and the least, after the best has been squeezed out. Don't allow yourself to be used, getting the least and the last, where God is not glorified. There is no profit.

Living to please and impress people is a prison that no one can be taken out of by anyone but by himself.

Any time, any where, what is more important is not what any one did or said, but what God is saying.

The strength of a man is not in his arrogance, but in his wisdom.

One who trusts in riches and one, who trusts only in human effort, will both reap confusion and frustration.

It really does not profit to say pardon my ignorance. But to sow knowledge in yourself is wisdom.

You can not inspire others if you can not confidently manifest or express what you have inside.

Teach your children to be responsible and to know that there are consequences for their wrong actions. Give them reasonable opportunities to deal with the consequences of their actions.

The greatest advice I can ever give to anyone is do not compromise the principles (will) of God no matter where you are.

Quietness prevents strife when you are in the midst of proud men.

Let the word of God be your counsellor.

If you can not take a stand against the evil you see, with wisdom and moral restraint, you can not make a difference.

In faith we are not afraid to act. We act and when we fail, we try again. When we come to maturity we are strengthened in faith.

It is a glorious thing for a man to hate injustice and abhor pride. It is praise worthy for him to love mercy and truth.

To be merciful to someone who is oppressed and afflicted is great wisdom. To the merciful God is merciful. But we do so with a sound mind. (With love Jesus said to the woman, "neither do I condemn you", and with a sound mind He said, "go and sin no more")

Wisdom is like a loving friend who cares compassionately about you. One who gives you good counsel and lead you to all goodness.

No matter how elevated you are you must still honour the good work of one who is not recognized by men. You must still honour the faithfulness of a poor man. You must respect the truth, not persons.

The best thing one can do for himself is to hold onto wisdom and never let it go a single day.

The judgement of people does not overthrow a man who trusts in the Lord. He will still prosper and the Lord will preserve him though he is condemned of man.

Wisdom is simple to one with understanding, but it is too high to one without understanding.

Knowledge is for the soul, and it brings exaltation.

There is knowledge that when a man has he becomes as bold as a lion. That is the knowledge of God.

When your faith is in the Lord you are not troubled by anything or anyone. You worry about nothing.

Never lean on people or put your trust in a man but in the Lord.

Don't trust in yourself to take yourself out of any trouble. Trust in the Lord to deliver you always.

See the target clearly and stretch your mind towards it.

Set your heart right with God and let your spirit be steadfast with God. Seek His will and declare His righteousness. Worship Him and give thanks to Him always. Be steadfast in His covenant by faith. (Psalm 78:8, 32, 37).

When you believe one day, satan is threatened. But he is really deeply troubled when you are steadfast in your faith in God.

Never forget the works of God (we are saved by His own work not our own). Never forget His signs and wonders. Remember His power and His might. (Psalm 78:42).

ABOUT THE AUTHOR

Born Philemon Khathutshelo Tshikota, Philemon grew up in a family of 5 children. He was born and raised in Rathidili, Louis Trichardt, South Africa. Later he moved to Johannesburg where he received his Bachelor of Business Administration Degree and Diploma in Information Technology from Cida City Campus. He has served as a leader for 9 years in Alleluia Ministries International (AMI), under the leadership of Pastor Alph Lukau, general overseer of AMI. Minister Philemon is a passionate writer who is endowed with wisdom and great insight.

Made in the USA
Middletown, DE
23 December 2020